POEMS FROM KOREA

D1827486

POEMS
FROM KOREA

FROM THE EARLIEST ERA
TO THE PRESENT

Compiled and translated by
PETER H. LEE

Foreword by Norman Holmes Pearson

London
GEORGE ALLEN & UNWIN LTD
Ruskin House   Museum Street

First published in Great Britain in 1974

© Unesco 1964, 1974

ISBN 0 04 808019 5

Originally published by The John Day Company, Inc., 1964. This revised edition first published by George Allen & Unwin Ltd and The University Press of Hawaii, 1974.

UNESCO COLLECTION OF REPRESENTATIVE WORKS
KOREAN SERIES

This book
has been accepted
in the Korean Series
of the Translations Collection
of the United Nations
Educational, Scientific and
Cultural Organization
(UNESCO)

Printed in Great Britain
by Unwin Brothers Limited
The Gresham Press
Old Woking Surrey

To the memory of Wallace Stevens, 1879–1955

Oh! Blessed rage for order, pale Ramon,
The maker's rage to order words of the sea,
Words of fragrant portals, dimly starred,
And of ourselves and of our origins,
In ghostlier demarcations, keener sounds.
—THE IDEA OF ORDER AT KEY WEST

ACKNOWLEDGMENTS

I would like to thank Sir Maurice Bowra, Daniel L. Milton, Norman Holmes Pearson, and René Wellek for their kind encouragement; Donald Keene for reading the Introduction; and Denise Levertov for having read through the entire manuscript and making many useful suggestions.

Acknowledgments are due to the editors of the *Beloit Poetry Journal, Monumenta Serica, Oriens Extremus, Orient/West* (Tokyo), *Poetry* (Chicago), and *T'oung Pao* for their permission to reprint groups of poems which first appeared in their journals; to the Istituto Italiano per il Medio ed Estremo Oriente for their permission to reprint all the twenty-five Old Korean poems which first appeared in my book, *Studies in the Saenaennorae: Old Korean Poetry* (Rome, 1959); and contemporary Korean authors for permission to translate their poems.

The excerpt from Wallace Stevens' essay "The Whole Man" quoted in Dr. Pearson's Foreword is from *Opus Posthumous* (Alfred A. Knopf, Inc.) and his letters are quoted with the kind permission of Mrs. Holly Stevens.

CONTENTS

Foreword, 11   Preface, 13   Introduction, 17

THE SILLA DYNASTY (57 B.C.–A.D. 935)

THE KORYŎ DYNASTY (918–1392)

THE YI DYNASTY (1392–1910)

TWENTIETH-CENTURY POETRY

FOREWORD

There is a good reason for Peter Hacksoo Lee to use a quotation from Wallace Stevens as the epigraph for his *Anthology of Korean Poetry*. Wallace Stevens was an older friend, and it was through Stevens that I first met him. Stevens wrote about Peter Lee in "The Whole Man." "Last week," he said in that essay, "I received a letter, greetings on my seventy-fifth birthday, from a young scholar, a Korean. When he was at New Haven, he used to come up to Hartford and the two of us would go out to Elizabeth Park, in Hartford, and sit on a bench by the pond and talk about poetry. He did not wait for the ducks to bring him ideas but always had in mind questions that disclosed his familiarity with the experience of poetry. He spoke in the most natural English. He is now studying in Switzerland at Fribourg, from where his letter came. It was written in what appeared to be the most natural French. Apparently they prize all-round young men in Korea, too. In his letter, he said, 'Seventy-five years is not a great deal, when one thinks that the poets and philosophers of the Far East, nourishing themselves only on the mist, have been able to prolong life up to one hundred and even one hundred and fifty years. Historians tell us that they have then been able to enter into fairyland, which is beyond our comprehension today.'

"That is my idea of a specialist," Stevens went on to say, "if these venerable men, by reducing themselves to skin and bones and by meditation prolonged year after year, could perceive final harmony in what all the world would concede to be final form, they would be supreme in life's most magnificent adventure. But they would still be specialists."

Peter Lee is indeed an "all-round" man, as a poet and scholar who can recognize and transmit the moods and tones of the final harmony of specialists. He is fluent in Korean, Chinese, Japanese, English, French, German, and Italian. His doctorate was earned, in German, from the University of Munich. He is able to define the nature of Korean poetry by recognizing what it is like and what it is not like. He has models to watch, and the experience of

11

poetry to guide him. "These poems," Stevens wrote about Lee's poetry in 1954, "are all singularly free from abstractions and perhaps that is why they are so moving and attractive. . . . All poems touch one with the reality of their poetry." Stevens might also have said that they show, as successful poetry should show, "the maker's rage to order words of the sea." The sea of natural wonder is everywhere in them. The final form is evident. Stevens wrote me later that he would write an Introduction to a collection of Lee's translations. "When you get around to doing this book, let me know a few weeks in advance, if you can, because I like to have plenty of time for everything." But the manuscript never reached him; there was not time enough, and Peter Lee had more to learn.

I have watched Lee's collection of Korean poetry develop, over the past decade, in comprehensiveness and the skill of his renderings. It is a remarkable achievement in introducing on this scale for the first time to a Western audience an important body of poetry and a national sequence of poets. They increase our literary resources. Their poems are "words of the fragrant portals."

—NORMAN HOLMES PEARSON

PREFACE TO THE SECOND EDITION

In reissuing this collection which has been out of print for some time, I have decided to let most of the poems stand in the form in which they first appeared. My theories of translation have changed considerably since the publication of the first edition almost ten years ago; I have therefore contented myself with correcting some errors or revising some passages in the light of recent Korean scholarship. I am grateful to George Allen and Unwin of London and the University Press of Hawaii for their heroic venture and to the Center for Korean Studies at the University of Hawaii for its generous assistance.

—Peter H. Lee

Honolulu, 1973

PREFACE

The poems contained in this book were translated between 1953 and 1962. The plan of the book was conceived during my stay in the Graduate School of Yale University, where I first felt it important that someone should introduce and elucidate Korean poetry to the West. Since that time I have worked at this anthology, which attempts to be at once comprehensive and representative. It includes all the pure native genres of vernacular poetry in Korea, but does not treat the poetry written in a language other than Korean. Many of my country's poets have ventured, from time to time, into classical Chinese, using Chinese verse-forms; their works have not been my concern. The best of our poetry has always been written in Korean, using native poetic genres. (It is not artificial to separate poetry written in Korean from poetry written in Chinese by the same author, as the relationships between the two are not as inseparable as in some equivalent cases in the West, such as Petrarch writing in Latin, Milton in Italian, and Rilke in French.) In this book, accordingly, Korean poetry is regarded as comprising all literary works by Korean writers in the Korean language.

My intention here is to bring Korean poetry close to the modern, non-Korean reader. Selections are made solely upon the basis of literary importance and are designed to demonstrate the diverse phases of Korean poetry. I have attempted to take a midway course between a literal and literary translation. I have also endeavored, if not always successfully, to give some slight impression of the rhythm of the original. The original form is kept in every respect except in the *sijo* translations. In most cases I have made it a six-line stanza, instead of original three-line stanza, for technical convenience; and when the refrains are not transferable into English and have no meaning even in Korean—i.e., incantatory refrains or such singing equivalents as "hey-nonny-nonny"—they are omitted and the number of lines in a stanza is thus shortened.

This anthology is possibly unique in that it covers a period of almost two thousand years and is the work of a single translator. It has obvious drawbacks. The variety and diversity in style and diction that is granted to any one translator might perhaps not be thought elastic enough to comprehend so wide a range of materials. On the other hand, Far Eastern poetry inclines in its very nature to be more formulaic and traditional than Western poetry, so that not only are themes repeated, but the style of a tenth-century poem may be closer to a poem of the eighteenth century than are, say, the styles of Villon and Mallarmé, who are in fact much closer in time. In other words, the individualistic tone of Western poetry is not present to the same degree in the poetry of the Far East. Indeed, sometimes a spurious variety is created by those anthologies of translations by several hands in which the diversity of styles is greater than the poems literally warrant; and this is likely when translators of distinguished but widely different sensibilities and periods are assembled between the covers of one volume.

The Introduction is designed to provide the reader with such historical, cultural, and literary background as is necessary for the appreciation of the poems themselves. It will, I hope, provide the reader with an understanding of the context in which these poems were originally framed. For further information I ask the reader to turn to my forthcoming *Korean Literature: Topics and Themes,* a short history of the vernacular genres of verse and prose in Korea.

The romanization of Korean names follows the McCune-Reischauer system.

—Peter H. Lee

Honolulu, 1964

16

INTRODUCTION

The Koreans, according to the Chinese chronicles, are "a people who enjoy singing and dancing." Many centuries before Christ, in the north, there were six tribes who spoke almost the same language and had the same customs and manners. They offered sacrifices to heaven in the first and tenth moons, and during these festivals the people gathered together and danced and sang. The three southern tribes, on the other hand, made offerings to gods in the fifth and tenth moons, and the people flocked together for these occasions and danced and sang far into the night. These gods were worshiped in spring and fall; in spring to pray for a prosperous crop and in autumn to give thanks for an abundant harvest. The center of the ceremony was communal worship of heaven, growing out of the collective consciousness of the communal mind. The patterned sense of community developed its proper rhythm in dance and song.

The quality of ancient Korean poetry was thus religious or magical. We conjecture that its norm was a few lines of simple language followed by a refrain. The language was incantatory, rich in its associative power and reference, rhythm and euphonies. It not only exerted a binding effect upon men, but upon gods and spirits as well. It was, first of all, a means of communication between gods and men. The magical power of words was believed in to such an extent that poetry was supposed to please gods, help avoid natural calamities, bring rain and stop the winds, and promote recovery from diseases. Primitive society was tribal and patriarchal, and primitive life was carried on in terms of communal values. Hence poetry, music, and dance, the three vital elements in religious services of ancient Koreans, were inseparable and indispensable. The earliest Korean poetry, insofar as we know it, was closely connected with Korean religion and was mainly composed of sacred hymns. It was a folk art that grew naturally out of their agricultural life.

Since then Korean poetry has been an essential part of Korean culture. The indigenous genre of vernacular poetry was first developed and perfected by the Silla people; the succeeding dynasties also invented and preserved other genres. Most important, however, is the fact that poetry in Korea is not a possession of a small coterie or class but of an entire people. Every man and woman was responsible for its birth and growth; its fortune was shared by every man and woman. Poets, although steeped in their own native tradition, had at the same time never neglected to receive and digest the great tradition of Chinese poetry. Poetry was considered as the most serious and intelligent of all arts, and its medium, the Korean language, as the glorious part of their heritage.

From the fourth century onward, three aristocratic kingdoms, Koguryŏ, Paekche, and Silla prospered on the peninsula. Unhappily, however, the earliest flowering of lyrical poetry in these kingdoms is known to us through the chronicles for the most part in terms of individual titles accompanied sometimes by the circumstances which prompted the composition of these poems; the texts in most cases have been lost. We have records of forty-one poems from Silla, five poems from Koguryŏ, and four poems from Paekche.

It was, however, in the kingdom of Silla that the first true vernacular poetry flourished. This was because, while Koguryŏ and Paekche were harassed by continual foreign invasions or internal disturbances, Silla was able to develop her indigenous culture in relative peace in an isolated corner of the peninsula. The native culture continued to grow, even after the importation of Buddhism. The influx of Buddhist culture provided the Silla people with an opportunity to recognize and cherish their own heritage and to attain a mature indigenous culture. Seventeen Buddhist poems out of twenty-five extant Old Korean poems are the testimony of the mature mind of the Silla people. Poets used Buddhism and its myths as their material, as Dante used Thomism for his. The sensibility is Korean, the form Korean, and the techniques as well. Great Master Kyunyŏ (917–973), though he wrote his poems after the pattern of the Buddhist hymns, Bhadra-caripranidhāna, or Vows on the Practices of Bodhisattva, was able to let the Korean sensibility seep through his works.

The most characteristic Silla institution was the hwarang which contributed largely to the advancement of the arts. The hwarang,

18

consisting of youths from aristocratic families, was a chivalrous organization whose function was to serve the country in times of emergency and to foster a sacrificial spirit for the sake of the country. Kim Yu-sin, who helped bring about the unification of the peninsula, was a *hwarang*. Thus members of the *hwarang* were called "the pillars of the state," "the paragons of youth," and "leaders of society." But they were not only gallant soldiers. In times of peace, they visited famous mountains and beauty spots to appreciate and to contemplate the beauty of nature. Among their favorite spots were the Diamond Mountains with countless peaks facing the Eastern Sea. Here spiritual cultivation was emphasized, and they learned on these occasions how to adhere to their principles, how to enlighten and correct one another, and how to become champions of public enlightenment. The *hwarang* also served as an important medium of liberal education, in which learning meant not only the reading of the classics, but also discussion and exchange of views and observations of the deeds of other members. In this manner, they would discuss poetry and music as they walked up and down the paths, not of a Lyceum, but of the Diamond Mountains or along the Eastern Sea. Many of them excelled in poetry and music, and many impromptu poems were attributed to them. The poet Siro, a member of the *hwarang*, praises his Master, Taemara, in one of the Silla poems. It is no wonder, then, that the *hwarang* should be praised as "national paragons" or "national geniuses" and not only as "the paragons of youth."

It is evident from our discussion why it was in Silla that the first polished form of vernacular poetry, the *Saenaennorae*, appeared. The *Saenaennorae* means "poems of the East," namely Korea, its own native songs in contrast with foreign songs, Chinese poetry, and covers in particular the fourteen poems in the *Samguk yusa* or *Remains of the Three Kingdoms* (c. 1285) and eleven devotional poems in the *Kyunyŏ chŏn* or *Life of the Great Master Kyunyŏ* (1075). On the basis of the existing poems, we may say that there are three forms in Old Korean poetry. The perfect development of a given theme on a dramatic plane was made possible by the last and most highly perfected of the three. It has two stanzas of four lines in which the main theme is developed, and a

19

stanza of two lines in which a summary of a thought that has been developed is given in the form of wishes, commands, or suggestions. This last stanza gives, so to speak, a conclusion to the poem, at times in a very sophisticated manner, and has an epigrammatic quality, memorable and quotable.

When we enter the Koryŏ dynasty, Buddhism loses the qualities of creativity and lucidity that marked Buddhism and Buddhist arts in Silla. The growth of Koryŏ was greatly retarded by the incessant invasions of the Khitans, Jurchens, and Mongols, and the coastal raids of the Japanese corsairs. Under the stresses of these invasions, the economy of Koryŏ was strained, her society crumbled, and the court decayed. Despite the decline of Buddhism, the Koryŏ people made a singular contribution to the technique of printing. They produced the complete Buddhist scriptures, the *Tripiṭaka*. This was an act of national piety, undertaken to win divine protection against the Khitan and Mongol hordes. The 81,137 wood blocks are preserved today in the Haein Temple in South Korea. A marvel in the realm of fine arts in Koryŏ was the celadon, which has been termed "one of the greatest triumphs of the potter's art." Highly developed artisans not only produced pale green celadon, but baked blue, glazed tiles. One royal pavilion was entirely roofed with such tiles.

Music and poetry were developed in such annual events as the lantern and harvest festivals which took place in the first (or second) and eleventh moons respectively. People gathered together, danced and sang, and popular poems were developed on such occasions. The form of poetry characteristic of this period is the *changga* or long poem. It is so called because of the refrain recurring at intervals, generally at the end of each stanza. This refrain in the *changga* is used to help achieve a certain mood in each poem, as in Provençal and Renaissance poetry. This character of the refrain is clear when we consider that the poems of this period were orally transmitted and their origin lay in folk songs or in the popular ballad. The refrain in the Koryŏ poems is, therefore, an indispensable element in chain verse like the *changga*.

Historical sources record sixty titles of Koryŏ poems, twenty with texts and forty without. However, authors of the *changga* characteristic of this period were all ordinary people. The *kisaeng*,

Korean female entertainers comparable to the Greek *hetaera*, played an important role in the literary world and left four poems of high literary merit. Love, the eternal theme in world literature, was the main subject during this period, and we are struck by the intensity of emotion and frankness of expression. Whether in the glow of peach blossoms, or in the chorus of orioles, or by the stream where they cleansed body and mind, or under the full September moon among chrysanthemums, or when they spent a long sleepless night, they were not ashamed to exalt love and its mystery or to reveal their sorrow or joy simply and frankly. These poems were usually sung to musical accompaniment, and found their place whenever men and women met together and entertained each other with songs. What should here be emphasized, however, is that the passion for decorum and order was not the only passion in Korea. Poets were not satisfied with the pale *vers de société* composed by the thousands in other countries. What was real to the poets was not a stylized feeling toward nature and life, but what the poet intensely felt, the quality of inner experience. This courage to live, courage to reveal the utmost quality of experience with spontaneity and frankness, was characteristic not only of the Koryŏ dynasty poets but also of the entire Korean sensibility.

The Yi dynasty, founded by General Yi Sŏng-gye in 1392, was a period of inventions and compilations, advancement and enlightenment. The period saw improvements in movable type, first invented in Korea about two centuries before Gutenberg. Most significant of all, however, was the invention of a purely phonetic alphabet in 1443 which was promulgated by Great King Sejong in the autumn of 1446. Great literary works began to be published; literature and the arts flourished. First of all, the new dynasty directed the compilation of existing court and popular music, and the composition of the new dynastic music. During the last decade of the fifteenth and in the beginning of the sixteenth centuries, two invaluable classics of Korean music were compiled by the Yi dynasty musicians. Eulogies praising the foundation of the dynasty appeared one after another, culminating in the great eulogy cycle consisting of 125 cantos (1445). The new literary genres rose one after another, and among these the most popular was the *sijo*, which came into being toward the beginning of the fourteenth century.

The origin of the *sijo* is not yet fully known, but the earliest author to whom extant *sijo* are attributed is U T'ak (1262–1342). Generally speaking, the *sijo* is a short, polished poem—more personal, specific, and local than the proverb—ending with a graceful, profound, and witty turn of thought. Yet the soul of the *sijo* is not wit, but sensibility. In Korea, the *sijo* was an art for the many, and every educated man and woman used this form for almost any purpose. Every topic, every mood, every style, was possible. It was, as a Renaissance critic described the epigram, "sweet, sour, bitter, and salt." A writer was not only familiar with its tradition and with its concentrated art, but was so deeply versed in it that he did not have to struggle to conform to its strict rules. In consequence, many *sijo* were composed *extempore*, ordinarily to be sung to a lute accompaniment. But the marvel is that they still show the marks of tradition and discipline, of grace and harmony. Thus the *sijo*, to the writers of the Yi dynasty, was an art in which words and music formed a single unit. A great body of the *sijo* was gathered in anthologies during the eighteenth and nineteenth centuries.

The norm consists of a stanza of three lines with fourteen to sixteen syllables in a line, the total number of syllables never more than forty-five. Internally this triplet is again divided into three sections: beginning, middle, and end. Each line has generally four syllable groups, but internally it can be divided into two groups of several syllables. A pause, equivalent to a caesura, comes after the second group of syllables in each line. In other words, it is a poem consisting of a three-line stanza, four feet in a line, and three to four syllables in a foot. Thus the basic form is as follows:

First line:	3	4	4	4/3
Second line:	3	4	4	4/3
Third line:	3	5	4	3

The *sijo* written toward the end of Koryŏ and the beginning of Yi were often occasional pieces. They were either retrospective or panegyric: retrospective ones written by the surviving retainers of Koryŏ, and panegyric ones by meritorious subjects of the new

22

kingdom upon the vastness of the royal works. Many political changes also inspired writers to lament disorder in the country and to display both their command of pathos and their versatility of style. On one occasion, a general sang of the victory of his army over the Jurchens. Among the soldier-poets Yi Sun-sin (1545–1598), a famous admiral whose victories turned the tide of war during the Japanese invasion (1592–1598), left several *sijo* of high literary merit. On other occasions kings and subjects sang of constancy and loyalty. The same period produced many social and political satires which were neither blunt nor unpolished, and were sufficiently brilliant and refined to be read as poetry.

In the sixteenth century, from the time of King Chungjong, scholar-poets came to be active on the literary scene. The two most famous Neo-Confucianists, Yi Hwang (1501–1571) and Yi I (1536–1584), wrote a *sijo* cycle in which they showed a keen appreciation of the beauties of nature. What they desired was to live in a hermitage among the mountains far from the din and bustle of the world. There were, however, two kinds of scholar-poets: those who had tried the official world and tasted bitter disappointment, and those aging government officials who intended to spend their later days in retirement. Their motives might be different, but they were one in their search for a quiet life among the settings of nature. When they met by the fountain or near the lake, they either devoted themselves to reading, or made friends with the morning flower or evening moon among the streams and stones. Thus their works were either learned and didactic, inculcating the teachings of ancient sages; or sentimental and escapist, singing of the hills and waters. The influence of the scholar-poets on the academic world was not slight. Encouraged by their nature poetry and by their use of the *sijo* form instead of conventional Chinese verse forms, students of Sung philosophy began to take a serious interest in this art.

The essence of the glorious tradition of the *sijo* was preserved and continued by Hwang Chin-i (c. 1506–1544), the greatest Korean poetess of all periods. She was a famous *kisaeng* at Songdo, and her fame in poetry and music was widespread in the capital. She was a master technician and knew how to develop the chosen image on a dramatic plane. Her images were always simple and sensuous, generally drawn from nature, but they were always chosen for analogy and double vision. Not only is natural imagery used as a metaphor of the speaker's emotion; nature herself was personified and allegorized to produce many levels of meaning. From this kind of symbolism comes a unique intensity.

> Blue mountains speak of my desire,
> Green waters reflect my Lover's love:
> The mountains unchanging,
> The waters flowing by.
> Sometimes it seems the waters cannot forget me,
> They part in tears, regretting, running away.

Here allegory is tinged with metaphysical and even religious overtones. Hwang Chin-i's perception and intuition of the great theme of mutability and the relationship between transcendence and immanence is rendered into sensuous visual images. Here she approximates, *mutatis mutandis*, the technique of the English Metaphysical poets. Her poetry is characterized by a wealth of symbolism, a metrical orchestration, a harmonious order of words, and finally a mastery and flawless development of theme.

The perfection of the *sijo* form was attained in the seventeenth and eighteenth centuries. Scholar-poets again played an important role in bringing this form of verse close to the public. When scholars raised their goblets, they were either "romantic" or philosophical. In the bamboo groves they lay, perceiving the final harmony of the world and the mystery of all created things. Their topics were often traditional, and they repeated familiar themes and moods: angling under the moon, "plowing among the clouds," sensuous contemplation of nature, praise of wine, ecstasy of love, sorrow of parting, complaint of desertion, beauty of friendship, fear of death, simplicity of country life, evanescence of life, and the like. At times they also took inspiration from Chinese writers such as T'ao Ch'ien (365–427), Li Po (701–762), Tu Fu (713–770), and the Sung dynasty poets. Themes may have been conventional, but their treatment and technique varied with each poet.

The master of the *sijo* form in the seventeenth century was with-

24

out doubt Yun Sŏn-do (1587–1671), who was perhaps the most versatile and inventive of all Korean poets. His lyrics are diverse in mood and method, and his mature poems abound in exquisite felicities. His vocabulary is simple yet forceful, common yet noble, and his masterly choice of the right word is unparalleled. Graceful and delicately varied rhythm was native with him, and every poem demonstrates new techniques and new tone. His poems number seventy-five altogether. Yun has been credited as a discoverer of the beauty of the Korean language. The hidden potentialities of the genre were thoroughly exploited by him, and certainly he brought not only progress, but perfection to the *sijo* art.

From the eighteenth century on, the *sijo* entered a new phase of development. This era corresponds to the period of the rise of the novel and of a middle class. In poetry it meant the retreat of the aristocracy who had dominated the literary scene for centuries, and the appearance of writers from the middle and lower classes. These new writers composed the *sijo* extempore, improvising freely to the existing tunes. Their language is simple and direct, and does not refrain from using rustic and unrefined vocabulary. Their tone is often hedonistic, and their works are rich in realism and humor. The famous anthologists Kim Ch'ŏn-t'aek and Kim Su-jang merit special mention not only as *sijo* poets, but as important musicians of the day. They stressed the musical quality of the *sijo*, composed both words and tunes, and sang their works to musical accompaniment before large audiences. Two poets who emerged toward the end of the nineteenth century, Pak Hyo-gwan and An Min-yŏng, have a singular place in the history of the *sijo*. They gave, so to speak, the final touch to this form of verse before the fall of the Yi dynasty. The *sijo* is still the favorite classical form of verse.

The *kasa* or discursive poetry is one of the new genres of the Yi dynasty and first appeared toward the middle of the fifteenth century. It is regarded as a modified form of the long poem of Koryŏ, but what differentiates it from the *changga* is that it has no stanzaic division, continues on like a chain, and has a tendency toward description and exposition rather than subjective lyricism. However, it has such characteristics as the use of accentuation and rhythm, of the caesura, and of balanced parallel phrases; and this is why one theory attempts to compare it with the Chinese *fu* or rhyme prose form. The norm of this new genre is a group of two four-syllable words which forms a single unit and is repeated in parallel form. The *kasa* poem varies in length from a poem longer than the *changga* of Koryŏ to several thousand lines. The anthologies record at least 300 of this kind, and the earliest extant poem of this type is the *Hymn to the Spring* by Chŏng Kŭg-in (1401–1481). Chŏng Ch'ŏl, Hŏ Nansŏrhŏn, and Pak In-no produced some of the finest examples in this form. From the eighteenth century on, the *kasa* became predominantly a popular form of poetry among women and common folk. This change was partly owing to the rise of the novel about the same time and the decline of verse genres. The *kasa* occupied, as it were, a middle position between prose and verse, and the rise of prose and of the middle class brought about changes in the inner form of the *kasa*, its subject matter, its audience, and its tone. Whereas the previous *kasa* dealt chiefly with elegant pleasures among nature, the beauties of the four seasons, the praise of civilization, and the like, the subject matter of the new *kasa* was daily life itself, life of both men and women of the middle and lower classes. The new poets and poetesses rejected the empty and idealistic world which the poet-philosopher or scholar-politician had once created; they relied solely on colloquial diction and conversational rhythm for effect, and welded written and spoken language into one. The *Song of the Lantern Feast* is a good example of this type dating from the eighteenth century.

Modern literature represents nearly a total break with the Korean past. As in China and Japan, a specifically modern type of expression developed much later than in Europe. Not until the beginning of the twentieth century did it make its appearance, and unlike European modern literature which continued the literary traditions of its own past, it tended to accept and imitate foreign examples. A rapid succession of literary movements and ideas in the short span of fifty years brought confusion to the literary world.

Despite the slowness of its start, modern Korean literature might have borne finer fruit if allowed to mature in a sympathetic and free atmosphere. The buds of the new literature were, however, soon nipped by an unseasonable frost when Korea lost her independence in 1910. During the period of thirty-six years from the Japanese annexation to the end of the Second World War, the new literature was forced to grow in the shadow of Japanese colonialism. It was doomed to be the literature of an exploited people. Denied the spirit of freedom and dynamism, the new literature in Korea became one of sorrow, reflecting a grief-stricken and despondent outlook. Without the indomitable spirit of the Korean people, Korean literature by itself could neither have preserved the Korean language—which embodies and manifests Korean tradition and culture—nor revealed the ultimate quality of the Korean sensibility. It was a triumph of this spirit that it preserved and continued the Korean language despite Japanese oppression.

The period of 1880–1905 is characterized by the introduction of Western learning and the translation of European literature into Korean. The next ten years, which may be termed the pioneering period, produced two great men of letters, Ch'oe Nam-sŏn and Yi Kwang-su. The former founded the *Sonyŏn* or *Children*, the first literary monthly in Korea; the new poetry movement may be said to have started with the publication of "From the Sea to Children" and three other poems by Ch'oe in the first number of this magazine published in October, 1908. Yi Kwang-su, on the other hand, was the first author to produce a novel of modern consciousness. Both Ch'oe and Yi were in the forefront of the patriotic movement before and after 1910; Ch'oe wrote the celebrated "Declaration of Independence" which kindled hope in millions of souls all over the country on the first day of March, day of the Independence Movement (1919).

Shortly before the unsuccessful and costly movement for liberation, Korean students studying in Tokyo published the magazine *Ch'angjo* or *Creation* in February, 1919. This publication's intent was to advocate national consciousness and to promote the development of new literature. It showed how far the new literary movement had progressed and represented a further step in the perfection of a vigorous new literary style. Two other important journals followed the *Ch'angjo*, *P'yehŏ* or *Ruins* in July, 1920, and *Paekcho* or *White Tide* in January, 1922. In this period of

27

experimentation the theories of new poetry were put into practice. Poets, keenly aware of the modern spirit, fostered—in the backward literary world of Korea—European literary movements which were not contemporary ones but those of the previous century. The poets, having rejected their own traditions and being unable to invent new conventions or a rational structure, were forced to resurrect past European movements and literary theories, in order to find conventions which would give coherence and meaning to their otherwise confused experience and practices. A contemporary of these groups, Kim Sowŏl (1903–1934), was a poet of nature and folk tradition, whose work was rich in local color. He sang of the rhythm and transcience of nature. His poems unfortunately defy translation, for their charm and power rely solely on the simplicity and freshness of the direct and intense language.

Meanwhile, general unrest grew among the literati after the Japanese invasion of Manchuria in September, 1931, and the rise of Nazism. As the pressure of Japanese censorship and colonial policies intensified, it became impossible for writers to express themselves freely. They were forced to become invisible, hiding their personalities and convictions behind their works of art. The only territory left for them to explore was the domain of pure poetry, which could transcend the steady aggravation of their situation. Poets found solace in the aestheticism of the Nineties and the perfection of techniques, remote from politics, philosophy, and the problems of society. Two poets of very different natures towered above their fellow writers—Chŏng Chi-yong and Kim Ki-rim, landmarks of the generation of the thirties. Chŏng, perhaps the best modern poet, has inspired—even to this day—a host of imitators and followers. His was a poetry of sensuous beauty, marked by a flawless diction and freshness of imagery which seldom have been surpassed. Some of his best poems depend for effect on the skillful use of onomatopoetic expressions which, if translated, lose their original charm and force. When he embraced Catholicism, his craftsmanship permitted him to produce the best Korean religious poetry of this century. A collection of his later poems, the *Paengnoktam* or *White Deer Lake* (1941), contains some of the jewels of modern poetry.

But not all poets of the thirties were of Chŏng's tribe. Some still suffered from the *fin-de-siècle* pangs. Others were lost in the forest of symbols, fondly explored the subconscious, or strode on the "invisible flux of consciousness." All in all, the garden of poetry was full of green carnations. In this moment, a school of "Intellectualists" headed by Kim Ki-rim, the second important poet of this period, resolved to set the garden in order. They found inspiration and support in the works of Pound, Eliot, Auden, and Spender. In order to replace the twilit dreamy world with concrete images, they first practiced Imagist poetry; later, in order to remedy their looseness of technique, this school, echoing Eliot, advocated the depersonalization of poetry. To illustrate the virtues of organization and accurate language, the "Intellectualists" also wrote satirical verse which purported to be a diagnosis of the unhealthy state of contemporary poetry. In criticism, the school hailed clarity and craftsmanship above all, condemned irrationality and sentiment in poetry, and asserted that objectivity and analysis should be the sole criteria of criticism.

With the outbreak of the Sino-Japanese War in 1937, the literary world faced the last stage of severe trials. Nationalist or anti-Japanese thought was not tolerated by the Japanese police, and the military encroached upon every literary activity. But writers did not succumb: instead they struggled to continue their art and, most important, to preserve the Korean language. The best means at their disposal was the practice of pure poetry. Many of them retired to the country, following the example of the ancient hermits. Literary productions increased in the midst of spiritual and cultural crises. Between 1937 and 1941, more than fifty collections of verse adorned the literary world, a clear manifestation of the determined love of writers for the Korean language and a reaction against Japanese attempts to undermine what was truly Korean. The role played by the journals *Munjang* or *Literature* (1939) and *Inmun p'yŏngnon* or *Criticism of Culture* (1938) in the development of contemporary poetry should not be overlooked. Through these magazines poetry was furthered and new figures were brought to the attention of the public. The chief discovery of this period was of a cluster of nature and folk poets writing, in the South, with remarkable virtuosity.

In 1941, the Sino-Japanese War developed into the Pacific War.

The Japanese, in order to suppress the identity of the Korean race, required Koreans to adopt Japanese names. Those who spoke the Korean language in public were seized and imprisoned. Two Korean newspapers were suspended on August 10, 1940, and the *Munjang* and *Inmun p'yŏngnon* were discontinued in April of the following year. Korean literature was driven underground. In despair, writers threw away their pens, and a dark period for literature ensued.

The political confusion after 1945 and the subsequent outbreak of the Korean War disrupted creative activities. Although some produced works of artistic merit, most efforts during the conflict were accounts of the horror and devastation of war. Meanwhile a series of significant events took place in the literary world. In 1954, the Korean Academy of Arts was established, and the Korean Chapter of the P.E.N. was organized to promote cultural exchange with the West. Several literary awards were instituted, and increasing opportunities were offered to writers by new literary journals. New names appear every year, yet it would be premature to evaluate the poetry written since the Korean War. But the period of experimentation seems to be over; and a new poetry which faithfully continues Korean traditions is in the making.

THE

SILLA DYNASTY

57 B.C.–A.D. 935

King Mu of Paekche
[600–641] [1]

A woman who lived on the shore of the South Lake near the capital had a child by the Dragon King. The child was named Chang, but people called him Mattung ("the youngest child"). His ingenuity was beyond compare, and he used to live by selling the Chinese yams he dug. Hearing of the perfect beauty of the third daughter of King Chinp'-yŏng (579–632), Princess Sŏnhwa, he shaved his head and came to the Silla capital. When he gave yams to the children there, they liked him and followed him. He then wrote a poem in the form of a nursery song, and had the children sing it. The song spread throughout the capital and reached even the royal palace. All the government officials were surprised, and they pleaded that the Princess be exiled from the capital. The Queen gave her a peck of gold and sent her on her way. As she traveled along, Mattung appeared, greeted her, and wished to escort her. The Princess did not know him, but had faith and joy in him, and allowed him to accompany her. When they made love, she learned that he was Mattung himself, and believed in the magical effect of the song. They went together to Paekche and were married. And eventually he became King, and was known as King Mu of Paekche.

SONG OF MATTUNG
c. 600

Princess Sŏnhwa,
Hoping a secret marriage,
Went away at night,
With Mattung in her arms.

Master Yungch'ŏn
[c. 579–632]

When the young men of the *hwarang*, leaders of the knights in Silla, made a trip to the Diamond Mountains, suddenly a comet appeared in the sky. The group hesitated to start until the poem by Master Yungch'ŏn could clear the comet away.

SONG OF THE COMET

There is a castle by the Eastern Sea,
Where once a mirage used to play.
Foreign soldiers came to admire this castle,
Torches were burnt, rockets were fired.

When Knights visited this mountain, and when
The moon zealously lit her lamp, and a star
With a long broomstick swept a path,
Someone said, "Look, there is a comet."

The moon has already departed.
Now, where shall we look for the long-tailed star?

Anonymous
[c. 635]

This ode praises the virtues of Yangji, who was a priest and a noted calligrapher. When he hung a sack on a priest's metal staff, the staff flew away and fell on the house of a benefactor of the temple. The people in the house saw it and filled the sack with alms. When the sack was full, it flew back to him. His dwelling was therefore called Sŏkchang ("Priest's Staff") Temple. His miracles were, as this one shows, beyond comprehension, and his ability beyond comparison. Once he built a pagoda out of bricks decorated with a thousand Buddhas of three Kalpas, and enshrined it at the temple and worshiped it. When he was carving the sixteen-foot Buddha for the Yŏngmyo Temple, he entered into meditation and concentrated on the work he was to accomplish. It is told that during the construction of this statue, men and women eagerly carried clay for the work, and this song is said to have been spread among the people and to have become popular because of this occasion. The compiler adds that this song was popular even in his day, and was sung when pounding rice and constructing buildings.

ODE TO YANGJI

We have come, have come,
Woe, woe to us—
We have come
To cultivate wisdom.

Kwangdŏk
[c. 661–681]

In the time of King Munmu (661–681), Monk Kwangdŏk formed a
warm friendship with Monk Ŏmjang. They used to promise each other
that the one who first attained the promised land would inform the
other. The former retired to a village named West Punhwang and
made shoes out of rushes; the latter had a hut built at Mount South
and followed the plow. One evening, when the sun cast a crimson
shadow and stillness settled in the pine grove, a voice spoke to Ŏmjang
from outside his hut: "I am going to the West. Fare you well, but fol-
low me soon." Having opened the window, he heard a heavenly music
far away in the clouds and saw the bright light gathering below. When
he went to visit his friend the following morning, he learned that
Kwangdŏk was dead. With the widow, he buried him at Kori, and
asked her if he might lodge in her house. She consented. One day
Ŏmjang, moved by a malicious impulse, proposed misconduct. She re-
buked him and further admonished him that it would be impossible
for him to enter paradise. Overwhelmed with shame, he went to his
master, Great Master Wŏnhyo, confessed his sin, and was supposed
to have attained the promised land.

PRAYER TO AMITĀBHA

O Moon,
Go to the West, and
Pray to Amitābha
And tell

That there is one who
Adores the judicial throne, and

35

Longs for the Pure Land,
Praying before Him with folded hands.

Can the forty-eight vows be met
If this flesh remains unannihilated?

Siro
[c. 692–702]

Knight Taemara was a son of Duke Suljong and served as a high administrator in the latter half of the seventh century. Siro, a dependent of his, was saved by his master when he had been transported to a distant place for forced labor.

ODE TO KNIGHT TAEMARA

All men sorrow and lament
Over the spring that is past;
Your face once fair and bright,
Where has it gone with deep furrows?

I must glimpse you, sir,
If I can, for an awesome moment.
My fervent mind cannot rest at night,
Faroff here in the mugwort-covered swamps.

An Old Man
[c. 702–737]

On his way to his new post at Kangnŭng, Duke Sunjŏng happened to eat his lunch by the beach. Looking at an azalea blooming on the cliff, his wife, Lady Suro, asked for the flower; but nobody dared to climb up to the top of the cliff. An old man leading the cattle—hearing her request—sang:

DEDICATION

If you would let me leave
The cattle tethered to the brown rocks,
And feel no shame for me,
I would pluck and dedicate the flower!

Sinch'ung

Before acceding to the throne, King Hyosŏng (737–742) played chess
with a wise man, Sinch'ung, under an oak tree. The King told his op-
ponent that he vowed by the oak never to forget him. After several
months, the King ascended the throne and awarded rewards to his sub-
jects in accordance with their merits; but he completely forgot about
Sinch'ung. Disappointed by the King, Sinch'ung composed this poem
and pasted it to the oak. Then the tree suddenly died. The King re-
gretted his poor memory, called him and conferred on him a title.
Then the tree, it is told, grew again.

REGRET
737

You said you would no more forget me
Than oaks would wither before the fall.
O that familiar face is there still,
The face I used to see and admire.

The moon in the ancient lake, it seems,
Complains of the transient tide, ebb and flow.
Your face I see no more, no more,
O the vain world, it hates and harasses me.

Master Wŏlmyŏng
[c. 742–765]

In the year 760, on the first day of the fourth moon, two suns appeared in the sky and remained for ten days. The King consulted astronomers, and they recommended that he pray to Buddha with flowers and songs. Thereupon the King had an altar built at the Chowŏn Hall, went to the Ch'ŏngyang Pavilion, and waited for the priest destined to perform this work. At that time the Master Wŏlmyŏng passed along the hill to the south. The King had him approach, ascend to the altar, and begin the ceremony. The Master said that he, being a member of the *hwarang*, leaders of the knights, was skilled only in the *Saenaennorae*, but not in Buddhist hymns. The King answered that since the priest was destined to the work, he could use the *Saenaennorae*. Thereupon the Master composed this poem.

TONNORAE: DEDICATION
760

O flowers strewn today
With a song. Since you attend
My honest mind's command,
You serve the laughing Maitreya!

In memory of his sister, he offered a mass for her soul with the dedication of this poem. At the very moment when it was recited a gust of wind came and blew the paper money of the offering away to the south.

REQUIEM

On the hard road of life and death
That is near our land,
You went, afraid,
Without words.

We know not where we go,
Leaves blown, scattered,
Though fallen from the same tree,
By the first winds of autumn.

Abide, Sister, perfect your ways,
Until we meet in the Pure Land.

Master Ch'ungdam
[c. 742–765]

Knight Kilbo, a member of the hwarang, leaders of the knights in Silla, was one of the friends of Master Ch'ungdam, a well-known poet in his time. This poem was known for its noble spirit and intense emotion, and the King himself is supposed to have praised it highly. Unlike the other poems of this group, it has no introductory note by the compiler.

ODE TO KNIGHT KILBO

The moon that pushes her way
Through the thickets of clouds,
Is she not pursuing
The white clouds?

Knight Kilbo once stood by the water,
Reflecting his face in the blue.
Henceforth I shall seek and gather
Among pebbles the depth of his mind.

Knight, you are the towering pine,
That scorns frost, ignores snow.

On the third day of the third moon of the year 765, King Kyŏngdŏk, standing on the Tower of the Kwijŏng Gate and looking around at his subjects, asked that a virtuous priest be brought to him. The first priest brought in was rejected by the King. Then another priest came—from the south in patched clothes and with a basket. The King greeted him

39

with a smile and received him into the Tower. Upon the King's questions, the priest replied that he was Ch'ungdam and that he used to go with tea to South Mountain on every third day of the third moon, and on the ninth day of the ninth moon, to pray to Buddha Elect. He was just on his way home from the Mountain. The King then asked him to compose a poem about statesmanship. After the poem was composed, the King praised it highly and wished to make him his chaplain; but the priest bowed twice and declined the King's offer.

STATESMANSHIP
765

The King is father,
And Ministers are loving mothers.
Subjects are foolish children;
They only receive what love brings.

The People are slow, often they live idly;
But once feed them love, and they thrive.
No one will desert the familiar land,
This is the way to govern a country.

Peace and prosperity will prevail if each—
King, minister, subject—live as he should.

Hŭimyŏng
[c. 742–765]

A woman named Hŭimyŏng in the village Han'gi gave birth to a boy; but when he was five years old, he became blind. The mother took him to the image of the Merciful Goddess, painted on the north wall of the Left Hall of the Punhwang Temple, and had him recite this poem and pray. The child gained his eyesight again.

HYMN TO THE THOUSAND-EYED GODDESS

Falling on my knees,
Pressing my hands together,

Thousand-Eyed Merciful Goddess,
I implore thee.

Yield me,
Who lack,
One among your thousand eyes,
By your mystery restore me whole.

If you grant me one of your many eyes,
O the bounty, then, of your charity.

Priest Yŏngjae
[c. 785–798]

The author of this poem was a man of mild disposition who excelled
in poetry. Once toward the end of the year, on his way to the South
Mountain, he met sixty thieves in the Taehyŏn Peak. The bandits
drew their swords and threatened him; but not displaying any sign of
fear, he told them his name. Since the bandits had heard of his repu-
tation as a poet, they asked him to compose an impromptu poem.
Moved by the poem that Yŏngjae composed, the bandits presented
him with two yards of silk. The priest laughed, declined it, and said,
since he knew riches were the root of Hell, he was about to abandon
the world and live in the mountains. When the priest threw the silk
on the ground with these words, the bandits threw away their swords
and spears, shaved their heads, and became monks and remained at
Mt. Chii all their lives. Yŏngjae was then ninety years old.

MEETING WITH BANDITS

My mind that knew not its true self,
My mind that wandered in the dark and deep,
Now is started out for bodhi,
Now is awakened to light.

But on my way to the city of light,
I meet with a band of thieves.

41

Their swords glitter in the bushes—
Things-as-they-are and things-as-they-are-not.

Well, bandits and I both meditate on the Law;
But is that sufficient for tomorrow?

Ch'ŏyong

This is probably the most famous of all Silla poems. Since peace and prosperity prevailed and the people rejoiced, King Hŏn'gang (875–886) went on a journey to Kaeunp'o. When he was starting back to his castle, black clouds suddenly arose, a dense fog thickened, and his men could not march forth. An inquiry was made, and a weatherman answered that this was all due to the anger of the Dragon King of the Eastern Sea, and that he could be calmed only by prayers in the temple. Accordingly, the prayers were offered and the sun reappeared. The Dragon King, much pleased by the offering, appeared before the King with his seven sons and praised his virtues. When the Dragon King returned to the sea after the song and dance, one of his sons did not accompany him, but instead followed King Hŏn'gang and came to the capital. He, the son of the Dragon King, called himself Ch'ŏyong, and married a beautiful woman from a good family. Seeing that she was extremely beautiful, an evil spirit transformed himself into a man and attacked her in her room while Ch'ŏyong was away. But Ch'ŏyong returned and witnessed the scene; and with calm he sang this song. His calm so impressed the evil spirit that it went away.

SONG OF CH'ŎYONG
879

Having caroused far into the night
In the moonlit capital,
I return home and in my bed,
Behold, four legs.

Two have been mine;
Whose are the other two?
Two had been mine;
No, no, they are taken.

42

Great Master Kyunyŏ
[917–973]

The contents of the poems are as follows: 1) the worship and veneration of Buddha; 2) the praise of Tathāgata; 3) the search for and offerings to Buddha; 4) repentance of sins and retribution in this life for the sins of a previous existence; 5) rejoicing in the welfare of others and in the reward of virtue; 6) the entreaty for the turning of the wheel of Law; 7) the entreaty for the coming of Buddha among the living; 8) the constant following of the way of Buddha; 9) the constant harmony with the living; 10) dedication of one's merits for the salvation of all living beings; 11) conclusion.

ELEVEN DEVOTIONAL FORMS

1

I bow today before the Buddha,
Whom I draw with the mind's brush.
O this body and mind of mine,
Strive to reach the end of ends.

He who is in every atom, He
Who presides over the four corners, He
Who overwhelms the world like the sea;
Would that I could always serve Him.

Idle body, mouth, mind,
Approach Him, be with Him, unimpeded.

2

"I devote myself entire to Buddha."
So speaks the tongue today eloquently.
Gush from the innermost of a spring,
O sea of inexhaustible voices and words.

We hail you, Saints,
We praise you, Teachers,

Of the Western Sea, virtuous kings,
Who exist even in dust and sand.

Would that my tongue could praise
An infinitesimal part of your virtue.

3

Stirring the ashes, lighting the lamp
Which burns at the altar, I pray:
That the wick reach Indra's heavens,
And the oil fill the sea.

This hand will strive for bodhi,
This hand will offer hands,
This hand will dedicate hands—
He who is here, He who is there.

Offerings are many: but what is equal
To the offering up of one's true self?

4

I have lived in fancy and vanity,
Strayed from the shores of light;
And the sins I have sinned,
They overflow, alas, the realm of All.

Good deed, thought, and word,
They banish the screen of evil.
Tell all the Buddhas, Confessor,
That today I truly repent.

When I enter Your kingdom, my penance
Ends: so all the evils.

5

As water and ice are of the same stuff,
Illusion and enlightenment are one.
Our Master defies both You and Me,
He and we the living are one.

Were we able to study His merits,
Were we able to master His ways,
Then would we obliterate self and other-self,
Then rejoice in the bliss of others.

Were we to follow in His footsteps,
How could the jealous mind be aroused?

6

To the boundless throne of Buddha
In the realm of dharma,
I fervently pray
For the sweet rain of truth.

Dispel the blight of affliction
Rooted deep in the ignorant soil,
And wet the mind's field
Where the good grass struggles to grow.

The mind is a moonlit autumn field
Ripe with the gold fruit of knowledge.

7

Although Buddhas who preside over the world
Have fulfilled the cause of their coming,
They will remain with us the living
Only when we rub and dedicate hands.

I have found the true friend
Whom I would follow night and day.
Have pity on these, Master, who wander
Upon the shores of illusion.

Were our minds pure and clean,
His image would be reflected there and shine.

8

I would fervently follow the vows
Which He initiated, established,

Attained through awesome labors,
With arduous progress, with vigor.

When this body turns to dust,
Even at the hour of my death
I would joyfully follow the vows
Unrolled through time by the teachers.

O mind that cultivates the way of Buddha,
Could it stray to the worldly way?

9

Sākyamuni takes the deluded as roots.
With His vow of great mercy,
He moistens the field of mind,
That the good in us be not withered.

I, who am one of the living,
Soon to be in the realm of dharma,
Would live and die with Him unshaken,
Praise Him as our Masters have praised.

The day we attained His wisdom,
He rejoices in our pure progress.

10

Would that my works of supererogation
Be turned to other's salvation,
Waking the deluded to the truth,
To the attainment of supreme Light.

When we realize the One and the Many,
Removed sins are jewels in His land;
Bodhisattvas too devoted their merits to others,
Fulfilled the pitying vow of great mercy.

He whom I worship and I are one;
Of one body and one mind.

11

When this world of the living runs out,
My vows too will have been acted out.
His merciful promise of awesome light—
O the boundless sea of his Truth.

Since we strive thus, thus do we work,
Each way we tread is a good way—
These are the Vows of Samantabhadra,
That our Masters took and fulfilled.

Then let us abandon this world, abandon
All, comprehend the Way that is His.

THE
KORYŎ DYNASTY

918–1392

King Yejong
[1079–1106–1122]

When King Chinhwŏn (892–935) of the Later Paekche dynasty ravaged the Silla capital in 927, T'aejo (877–918–943) of Koryŏ was greatly angry, took the field in person, and attacked Chinhwŏn at Mt. Kong, northeast of Taegu. The chances were against T'aejo, and the Chinhwŏn army surrounded him. The King was saved only by the desperate resistance offered by General Sin Sung-gyŏm, together with Wŏn Po and Kim Nak. When King Yejong in the tenth moon of the fifteenth year (1120) of his reign visited the p'algwanhoe ("harvest festival") at Sŏgyŏng, he saw the play of two masks on horseback. The King thought it strange, and inquired about it. Upon learning that they were the images of two generals, Sin and Kim, the King was deeply moved by their heroism and loyalty and honored them with a royal poem of eight lines.

DIRGE
1120

Loyal hearts that saved your King,
You go heavenward in bright honor.
Though the breath of life left your bodies
You were true to your duty.

O good men, brave and beautiful,
It is not hard for me to believe
That traces of fidelity remain,
Remembering how you preferred death to shame.

Chŏng Sŏ
[c. 1151–1170]

The poet who composed "Regret" was a favorite subject during the time of King Injong (1109–1123–1146). Upon the enthronement of King Ŭijong (1127–1147–1170–1173), he was banished from the capital to Tongnae as the result of party strife at court. At the place of exile, Chŏng composed this poem and sang it to the lute whose tone was described by the annalists as moving and sad.

REGRET

My mind that has thought of you and wept
Is like a bird in a lonely hollow.
The waning moon will know, and morning stars,
That their slanders were untrue and vain.
Your soul, my Lord, be there where mine drifts.
Who has opposed, insisted shamelessly?
I have committed no sin against you.
Alas, all that they told of me was slander.
Have you already wholly forgotten me?
Show favor to me, I entreat you, Lord, I pray.

Anonymous
[c. 1213–1259]

After the event of the year 879 in which Ch'ŏyong drove away the evil spirits (page 42), his mask was used by the people for the same purpose of expelling demons. On New Year's Eve, this choral dance was performed at court to exorcise evil spirits from the country.

SONG OF CH'OYONG: A CHORAL DANCE
FOR EXORCISING DEMONS

Prologue   In the reign of Silla, calm and bright,
Lived Ch'ŏyong, son of the Dragon King,
Inheritor of the virtues of Rahu.[1]
With him the great and mysterious,
We the living never had a word.

52

He disperse the three calamities,[2] the eight
difficulties.[3]

First Chorus   O his handsome mask, noble bearing,
Head, slightly inclining, adorned with flowers,
The broad brow that manifests longevity,
Long eyebrows, like those of a brave elephant;
Perfect eyes, clear and kindly;
Happy ears, garden of excellence;
Pink face of peach blossoms;
And having smelt five incenses, his high nose.
Indulgent mouth, as though drunk on fortune,
Teeth, like white jade or porcelain,
Chin, slightly curved, happily,
Shoulders, stooped under the Seven Treasures,[4]
Sleeves, hanging down, flooded with joy,
His breast, endowed with wisdom and wit,
Stomach, full with the good and lucky.
Pink sash about his narrow waist,
Legs that walked through the world at ease,
And his feet, to what a tune they danced!

Second Chorus   Who has made, who has made,
Without a needle, without thread,
Who has created Prince Ch'ŏyong?
Many have created him, built him,
Twelve kingdoms put him together.
Many have created Prince Ch'ŏyong.

Demon   Crab apples, green plums, come,
Come out to tie my sandals.
If you do not, I will curse you.

Second Chorus   Having caroused far into the night
In the moonlit capital,
I return home and in my bed,
Behold, four legs.

Two have been mine;
Whose are the other two?

People	Think now, Ch'ŏyong sees you,
	O demon, he will cut you to pieces.
	What shall we offer you, Prince Ch'ŏyong,
	Thousands of gold pieces, the seven treasures?
Ch'ŏyong	Not the gold, nor the treasures,
	Catch me that demon, catch him.
Demon	Over the field, over the water,
	Avoid Ch'ŏyong, far away.

Unknown *Kisaeng*
[c. 1275–1308]

"The Turkish Bakery" purports to be by a *kisaeng* (Korean female entertainer) and dates from the time of King Ch'ungnyŏl. This was a time when popular songs and music flourished, with the encouragement of the King himself, who gathered musicians and dancers from all over the country for his entertainment. From the contents of the poem, critics consider it as a city folk song of the day rather than as a poem of definite authorship. In the original the fifth and seventh lines in each stanza are an imitation of drum sounds carrying no definite meaning.

THE TURKISH BAKERY

I go to the Turkish shop, buy a bun,
An old Turk grasps me by the hand.
If this story is spread abroad,
You alone are to blame, little doll on the shelf.[1]
I will go, yes, go to his bower;
A narrow place, sultry and dark.

I go to the Samjang Temple, light the lantern,
A chief priest grasps me by the hand.
If this story is spread abroad,
You alone are to blame, little altar boy.

I will go, yes, go to his bower:
A narrow place, sultry and dark.

I go to the village well, draw the water,
A dragon within grasps me by the hand.
If this story is spread abroad,
You alone are to blame, O pitcher.
I will go, yes, go to his bower:
A narrow place, sultry and dark.

I go to the tavern, buy the wine,
An innkeeper grasps me by the hand.
If this story is spread abroad,
You alone are to blame, O wine jug.
I will go, yes, go to his bower:
A narrow place, sultry and dark.

Anonymous

An anonymous poem of sixty-five lines, the "Ode on the Seasons" is divided into thirteen four-line stanzas with a line of refrain at the end of each stanza. The first stanza is a panegyric prologue, and the following twelve stanzas are devoted to each of the twelve months of the year according to the lunar calendar. "Tongdong Dance," together with the choral dance of Ch'ŏyong, was performed on New Year's Eve in the beginning of the Yi dynasty.

ODE ON THE SEASONS

With virtue in one hand
And happiness in the other,
Come, come you gods,
With virtue and happiness.

The river in January
Now freezes, now melts.

The changing skies.
I live alone.

You burn like a lantern
In the February moon.
Burn like the bright lantern
That shines upon the world.

In the last day of March
Plums are in full bloom.
O magnificent blossoms,
How I envy you!

In April the orioles
Come singing on time.
But you, my clerk,
You forget bygone days.

On the feast of the irises
I brew healing herbs.
I offer you this drink—
May you live a thousand years.

On a June day I am like
A comb cast from a cliff.
Once I followed you,
I thought you were mine.

For the feast of the dead,[1]
I prepare dainties of land and sea,
And pray in this midyear day,
That we may be always together.

Under the full moon
Of the midautumn festival [2]
I am lucky to be near you
On the day of the Harvest Moon.

O season of chrysanthemums
In the ninth day of the ninth moon,
Drunk from wine, drunk from flowers,
Take care, love, be well and strong.

In frosty October
You are handsome as the laden tree.
But once the tree is cut down,
What will become of my love?

On a long November night
I lie on a dirt floor
With only a sheet to cover me.
O troubled heart, night without you.

In December I carve for you
Chopsticks from pepperwood:
An unknown guest holds them.
O bitter December!

Unknown Kisaeng

The "Song of P'yŏngyang" is a dramatic lyric by a kisaeng, consisting of two twelve-line stanzas and an eighteen-line stanza. Eight lines in the first and second stanzas and twelve lines in the third stanza are a kind of refrain serving to keep the text to the musical tune. The second stanza seems to have been popular in itself, apart from the entire poem, and recurs as the final stanza in the "Song of the Gong." The poem became a political issue during the reign of King Sŏngjong (1457–1470–1494) and was officially condemned as vulgar.

SONG OF P'YŎNGYANG

Although P'yŏngyang is my home and capital,
And the walls have all been repaired,
If I must part from you, be left behind,
I'll stop spinning, and stop weaving,
Follow my own love with salt tears.

Were the pearls to fall on the rock,
Would the thread be broken?
If I parted from you for a thousand years,
Would my heart be changed?

Not knowing the Taedong that flows on,
You pushed the boat off, O boatman.
Not knowing the sorrow that kills me,
You had him board the ferry, boatman.
Once he has crossed that awesome water,
He will pluck some other flower.

Anonymous

The "Song of Green Mountain" is written in eight four-line stanzas with the refrain at the end of each stanza, "yalli-yalli yallasyŏng yallari yalla," which is omitted in the translation.

SONG OF GREEN MOUNTAIN

Let us live in the green mountain,
With wild grapes and wild thyme,
Let us live in the green mountain.

With cry and moan
The birds fly overhead.
Tremendous sorrow nests in me
And cries and moans after I wake.

The birds fly over,
My plow is blunt.
The birds fly crying
Across the water.

I have spent the day.
But in this deserted place
Where no man comes or goes
How am I to pass the night?

At what place is this stone thrown?
At what person is this stone thrown?
Here where no man loves or hates,
What if I stumble on the stone!

Let us live by the loud sea,
With seaweeds and cowries,
Let us live by the neighing sea.

While you are turning the corner,
While you are going to a kitchen,
Listen to the stag fiddling,
Perched on a bamboo pole.

On the way to the sea I brew
Strong wine in a round jar.
A gourd-shaped leaven chases me and
Begs me to stay here; what now?

Anonymous

The "Song of the Gong" is an anonymous hymn which sings of an un-
broken line of kings and prays that the lives of kings be coeval with
heaven and earth. The poem offers a series of impossibilities, and then
claims that if these are ever resolved, as the refrain states, then only—
not before—do we part from the virtuous lord, our King.

SONG OF THE GONG

The King reigns; ring the gong.
In this age, calm and lucky,
Let us, let us live and love.

In a sand dune, fine and plain,
Let us plant roasted chestnuts, five pints.
When the chestnuts shoot and sprout,
Then we'll part from the virtuous lord.

Let us carve a lotus out of jade,
And graft the lotus in the stone.
When it blossoms in the coldest day,
Then we'll part from the virtuous lord.

Let us make an iron suit of armor,
Stitch the pleats with iron thread.
When it has been worn and is spoilt,
Then we'll part from the virtuous lord.

Let us make an iron ox, and put him
To graze among the iron trees.
When he has grazed all the iron grass,
Then we'll part from the virtuous lord.

Were the pearls to fall on the rock,
Would the thread be broken?
If I parted from you for a thousand years,
Would my heart be changed?

Unknown Kisaeng

"Winter Night" is a love poem of thirteen lines with no stanzaic division, of which the third line is a refrain. The translation does not attempt to reproduce this form. Together with "The Turkish Bakery," it was mentioned in the *Sŏngjong Annals* (1499) as vulgar in content and as being that which pleases men and women.

WINTER NIGHT

The sleet falls thick and fast;
Do you come, false love, who made me
Lie awake for half the night?
Are you crossing the pass
Where the wind cries in the bushes?

Fires of hell or thunderbolts
Will soon consume my body.

Fires of hell or thunderbolts
Will soon consume my body.

On what wild mountain shall I seek you?
I will do anything, anything you say,
The this and the that, whatever you ask of me.
I will follow you anywhere, I swear.

Anonymous

"Maternal Love" is an anonymous poem, and some literary historians
question its Koryŏ origin. Despite the scarcity of reference materials
on it, the vocabulary and its syntax and rhythm would seem to indi-
cate that it is a Koryŏ product.

MATERNAL LOVE

Spade too is an edged tool;
But in sharpness sickle certainly wins.
Father is father of man;
But in love the mother surely surpasses.
Yes, his indeed cannot be more than hers.

Unknown Kisaeng

In the original, "Will You Go?" consists of four two-line stanzas with
a refrain at the end of each stanza.

WILL YOU GO?

And will you go away?
Will you thus forsake me,
Leave me, and go away?

How can you leave me so
That loved you every day,
How can you leave me so?

I could cling to you, stop you,
But fear you would never return,
Scared by my salt tears.

Go, then, I'll let you go.
But return soon, soon return,
As easily as you leave me now.

Unknown *Kisaeng*

"Spring Overflows the Pavilion" is again an anonymous love poem. Its passionate, sensuous tone is probably the reason why the poem was condemned by the Yi dynasty annalists.

SPRING OVERFLOWS THE PAVILION

Were I to build a bamboo hut on the ice,
Were I to die of cold with him on the ice,
O night, run slow, till our love is spent.

When I lie alone, restless, vigilant,
Only peach blossoms wave over the west window.
You have no grief, welcome the spring breeze.

I have believed those who vowed to each other:
"My soul will follow yours forever."
Who, who persuaded me this was true?

"O duck,[1] beautiful duck, why do you come
To the swamp, instead of the shoal?"
"If the swamp freezes, the shoal will do."

A bed on Mt. South, a jade pillow, gold brocade,
And beside me a girl sweeter than musk,
Let us press our hearts together, our magic hearts.

U T'ak
[1262–1342]

Writer of the first extant *sijo*, he was a noted metaphysician and interpreter of the *Book of Changes*. Two poems are attributed to him, and from their content are believed to have been written toward the end of his life.

> East winds that melt the mountain snow
> Come and go, without words.
> Blow over my head, young breeze,
> Even for a moment, blow.
> Would you could blow away the gray hairs
> That grow so fast around my ears!

> Sticks in one hand,
> Branches in another:
> I try to block old age with bushes,
> And frosty hair with sticks:
> But white hair came by a short cut,
> Having seen through my devices.

Yi Cho-nyŏn
[1269–1343]

The twenty-eighth ruler of Koryŏ, Ch'unghye (Putaširi), was afforded a rare privilege; he held the throne twice: 1331 and again 1340–1344. He was addicted to sensual pleasures and failed to fulfill his kingly duties. Outspoken in his loyalty and devoted to the cause of duty, Yi censured the actions of the King on every occasion, urging him to labor for the welfare of the people. A frequent visitor to the inner palace, every time the King heard his footsteps, he would send away his catamites, sit straight, and await Yi's reprimands. His advice was, however, not heeded, and Yi resigned in protest to spend the remainder of

63

his days at home. He was posthumously made a marquis by King Kongmin (Bayan-temür, 1330–1352–1374).

> White moon, white
> Pear blossoms, the Milky Way
> White across the sky.
> An ignorant bird
> Repeats and repeats its song,
> Not noticing
> The sorrow of spring.
> Too much awareness is a sickness;
> It keeps me awake all night.

Chŏng Mong-ju
[1337–1392]

One of the canonized and most worshiped sages of Korea, Chŏng passed the civil service examination with highest honors in 1360, and in 1367 rose to be a professor of the National Academy. He was a skilled politician and was sent to China as envoy. When General Yi Sŏng-gye, founder of the Yi dynasty, was about to ascend the throne, Chŏng formed an opposition party and secretly plotted to overthrow him. T'aejong, the fifth son of the general, was anxious to remove the opposition and gave a feast in honor of Chŏng in order to detect the latter's intentions. Exchanging a cup, Chŏng sang this poem which showed unshakable determination and loyalty to the Koryŏ dynasty. Thereupon T'aejong sent assassins and had Chŏng killed on Sŏnji Bridge in Kaesŏng. The bridge is still dyed with red, supposedly from the blood shed by Chŏng when he was murdered. This poem is universally known to all Koreans, is set to music, and is an indispensable anthology piece.

> Were I to die a hundred times,
> Then die and die again,
> And all my bones no more than dust,
> My soul gone far from men,
> Yet still my red blood, shed for you,
> Shall witness that my heart was true.

Mother of Chŏng Mong-ju
[mid-fourteenth century]

Like the mother of Mencius, she was supposed to have devoted her love and energy to the education of her son, and she is famous for this poem alone.

> Do not, O do not go, eastern egret,
> Among the crows tearing and cawing.
> Angry crows, they will hate you,
> Jealous of your white feathers.
> Do not stain your innocent self
> That the blue waves have washed.

Yi Saek
[1328–1396]

One of the three most important scholars at the end of the Koryŏ dynasty, he passed the imperial examination at the Mongol court in 1354 and held the positions of Hanlin Academician, Special Drafting Official of the Secretariat, and Compiler of National History. Upon his return to Korea, he served as Compiler in the Office of Historiography and administrated state affairs for twenty years. When he was called to service after the dynasty had changed, he refused to take office and remained faithful to the former dynasty. The commentators add that "the tree of the perfect plum" refers to the royal house.

> Rough clouds gather around the valley
> Where the snow slowly melts.
> Where is the tree of the perfect plum,
> In what lowland, what hollow?
> I have lost my way, alone,
> In the setting sun.

Kil Chae
[1353–1419]

A famous scholar considered to be the first advocate of Sung philosophy in Korea. After the fall of Koryŏ, he refused the honors bestowed upon him by the king of the Yi dynasty (1400) and lived concealed in the country. His last years were devoted to education, and many of his disciples later became noted scholars. Often, overwhelmed by pent-up grievances, the poet visited the former capital, Songdo (modern Kaesŏng). The sight of the royal palace where once he used to serve carried him back to the old days. Recalling the past, he sang:

> On horseback, I visit Kaesŏng,
> The capital for five centuries.
> Hills and waters are ever the same;
> But could we list our heroes' names?
> Oh, golden age, is it a dream
> That once we praised peace in our songs?

Yi Chon-o
[1341–1371]

Little is known of him except that he passed the civil service examination in 1360. Here the allusion to clouds refers to villainous courtiers who, forgetful of their duty to the country and people, indulged themselves in obtaining their personal ambitions and comforts.

> Who says clouds do not plot treason?
> Floating in mid-air, high,
> Waywardly,
> Idly,
> For what reason do they cover
> The bright light of the day?

Ch'oe Yŏng
[1316–1388]

High General of the Army, who never lost a battle. He defeated the Jurchens, destroyed the Japanese corsairs in the southern coast, and subjugated Cheju [Quelpart] Island. When the army of Yi Sŏng-gye marched back from the Yalu River, he was transported to Ch'ungju and was killed by the Yi party. Everyone shed tears at his death, as he was one of the bravest and greatest generals in Korean history.

> Mounting a swift steed,
> Well fed, groomed,
>
> A brilliant sword in hand,
> Well ground, polished,
>
> I would repulse the invading foe,
> Strong in war, brave in death.

Hongjang

Little is known of this kisaeng at Kangnŭng except that she was popular toward the end of the fourteenth century.

> The moon shines into Hansŏng arbor,
> Water is calm at Kyŏngp'o Terrace.
> Gulls wander about as they always do,
> Searching for bygone days.
> But our Lord who has left us,
> Why does he not return, why?

THE

YI DYNASTY

1392–1910

Wŏn Ch'ŏn-sŏk

[c. 1401–1410]

He became a chinsa ("Doctor in Letters") in the early part of the four-teenth century, but soon left the capital and lived hidden in the coun-try, because the royal court was upset with political upheavals toward the end of the Koryŏ dynasty.

> Rise and fall is a destiny turning;
> The palace site is overgrown with weeds.
> Only a shepherd's innocent pipe
> Echoes the royal works of five hundred years.
> Stranger, keep back your tears
> In the setting sun.

Hwang Hŭi
[1363–1452]

He served as Chief State Counselor for eighteen years at the begin-ning of the Yi dynasty. Quiet and broad-minded, handsome and bril-liant, he was loved by the people as a wise statesman.

> Spring has come to a country village;
> How much there is to be done!
> I mend a net and
> A servant tills the fields and sows;
> But who is to pluck the sweet herbs
> That grow on the back-hill?

> In the valley of jujubes red and ripe,
> Chestnuts burst open and fall.
> Crabs move and mutter in the mud,
> They crawl in the rice paddies.
> Let's buy a sieve and strain new wine,
> Drink, and test the season's joys.

71

Kim Chong-sŏ
[1390–1453]

Statesman, general, and historian, Kim Chong-sŏ passed the civil service examination in 1405. From 1443 on, he—as governor of northern provinces—often subjugated the Jurchens. Climbing on the top of Mt. Paektu on the Korean-Manchurian border, he sang this heroic poem:

> Wintry winds punish the dead branches,
> The moon hangs high and cold over the snows.
> On nights like this I pace the fortress walls,
> My mighty sword in hand.
> Alas, nothing opposes me; only
> My fierce voice shakes the land.

Sŏng Sam-mun
[1418–1456]

One of the Six Martyred Ministers of King Tanjong (1441–1453–1455–1457). When King Sejo (1417–1456–1468) forced the abdication of his young cousin Tanjong, Sŏng and others plotted the latter's restoration. They were punished with death, and their beloved sovereign also died a cruel death in his place of exile. In a crucial moment, the poet expressed his determined loyalty to the memory of his lord.

> Were you to ask me what I'd wish to be
> In the world beyond this world,
> I would answer, a pine tree, tall and hardy
> On the highest peak of Mt. Pongnae,
> And to be green, alone, green,
> When snow fills heaven and earth.

I scan Mount Shou-yang,
Lament the sages, Po I and Shu Ch'i.[1]

They would rather have starved to death
Than pluck the wild bracken here:
Even though it is an innocent weed,
Does it not grow in the usurper's soil?

Chŏng Kŭg-in
[1401–1481]

He passed the final civil service examination in 1453 but retired to a
country village when Sejo usurped the throne from his young cousin.
He was awarded the posthumous title of Minister of Rites.

HYMN TO THE SPRING

What do you think of this life of mine,
You who are buried in red dust,[1]
Do I match the dead in love of nature?
I am not the only man beneath the skies:
But the pleasures of the hills are mine.
In a thatched hut before a stream,
Among the dense thickets of pine and bamboo,
I play host to the winds and the moon.

Winter left us yesterday; look,
Peach and apricot blossoms in the sunset.
Willows and plants are green in the rain.
As if in marks of a chisel,
As if in strokes of a brush, the hand
Of the Creator is everywhere, gay and extravagant.
The graceful birds in the wood
Drunk with spring time, flirt and sing.

Nature and I are one; the same pleasure
As I go out through the brushwood door,
As I sit in the arbor, as I walk and recite.
Days pass quietly among hills and waters;

But flavor is there—who knows it better than I!
Let's climb a hill, friends, go to the sea;
Today, walk on the green grass,
Tomorrow, bathe in the I River; [2]
Gather ferns in the morning,
Go angling in the evening, and
Strain wine through a coarse turban.
Let's drink it turn by turn, keeping count
Of our cups with plucked flowers; let
Gentle breezes cross the water, scatter
Fragrance in cups, strew petals on clothes.
Let me know when a flagon is emptied.
I dispatch a boy to a tavern, put it
On his shoulder; a stick leads me.
Humming a verse, we reach a stream and
Wash our cups on the sandy beach.
Then suddenly peach blossoms float down
From the fairy land of T'ao Ch'ien. [3]
Green hills over there must mark the place.
Between the pines in a narrow lane,
Our arms full of azaleas, we reach the hill;
Sitting on clouds, we scan the budding villages.
Smoke, mist and sun weave a brocade
Over adorned fields that once were gray.
I shun riches, I avoid a title.
Apart from the clear breeze and bright moon,
Who, who else is my friend?
With a handful of rice and a gourdful of water, [4]
Nothing distracts me, nothing diffuses my wit.
Well, what do you say, my friends,
To the prospect of a hundred years of delight?

Yi Chŏng
[1454–1488]

The elder brother of King Sŏngjong, he was well versed in literature, and spent a pastoral life in the north of Koyang.

> Night comes to the autumn river,
> The water is cold;
> Even the fish are sleeping,
> In vain I drop a line.
> Cold moonlight on the deck,
> Return, my empty boat, return!

King Sŏngjong
[1457–1470–1494]

The ninth king of the Yi dynasty excelled in poetry. He was a brilliant sovereign, encouraged learning, and cared much about the education of the people. He granted lands to the National Academy and provincial institutions and ordered the compilation of *General Mirror for the Eastern Country* and a compendium of Korean geography. He lived simply, tilling his fields himself, and his Queen raised silkworms. The following poem is addressed to one of his favorite ministers who was about to leave the court.

> Stay:
> Will you go? Must you go?
> Is it in weariness you go? From disgust?
> Who advised you, who persuaded you?
> Say why you are leaving,
> You, who are breaking my heart.

Kim Ku
[1488–1534]

A famous calligrapher and Taoist. One evening, as he was reciting some classics, someone knocked on the door of the Jade Hall. It was King Chung-jong (1488–1506–1544) himself with his attendants, and the King told Kim that he could not but share the joy of a scholar in a moonlit night. The King added that on such a night they should associate as friends, not as sovereign and subject, and offered him a cup of wine. At the King's request, Kim composed two poems, one of which is given here.

> Until the short legs of the duck
> Become long as a crane's—
> Until the crow becomes white,
> White as an eastern egret—
> Enjoy enduring bliss,
> Forever.

Kim Chŏng-gu
[c. 1495–1506]

Kim flourished under Tyrant Yŏnsan'gun; another source ascribes the poem to Yi Chung-jip.

> Who says I am old?
> Is an old man this way?
> Heart welcomes sweet flowers,
> Laughter floats over fragrant cups:
> But what can I do, what can I say?
> My hoary hair floats in the spring wind.

Sŏ Kyŏng-dŏk
[1489–1546]

He was born into a poor family in Kaesŏng but never resented his poverty. He hid himself in Mt. Sŏnggo and spent his life with books. Hwang Chin-i, the most famous Korean poetess, was his pupil, and in this poem the poet expressed his longing for her.

> My mind is foolish,
> And all that I do seems vain.
> Who would come to the deep mountain
> With its thick clouds, fold upon fold?
> I look to see whether you come by chance,
> Whenever the fallen leaves rustle in the wind.

Hwang Chin-i
[c. 1506–1544]

The most famous and the most accomplished of all Korean women poets. She lived in Songdo and had a host of admirers around her; her fame reached its zenith during the reign of King Chungjong. Her immense virtuosity appears most effectively in her love poems tinged with a philosophical tone.

> I cut in two
> A long November night, and
> Place half under the coverlet,
> Sweet-scented as a spring breeze.
> And when he comes, I shall take it out,
> Unroll it inch by inch, to stretch the night.

> Do not boast of your speed,
> O blue-green stream running by the hills:
> Once you have reached the wide ocean,
> You can return no more.

Why not stay here and rest,
When moonlight stuffs the empty hills?

———————

Mountains are steadfast but the mountain streams
Go by, go by,
And yesterdays are like the rushing streams,
They fly, they fly,
And the great heroes, famous for a day,
They die, they die.

———————

Blue mountains speak of my desire,
Green waters reflect my Lover's love:
The mountains unchanging,
The waters flowing by.
Sometimes it seems the waters cannot forget me,
They part in tears, regretting, running away.

Song Sun
[1493–1583]

After graduating as chinsa, he served under Kings Chungjong and Myŏngjong (1534–1546–1567). He then retired to the country and spent his life writing. The third poem is said to be a lament on the 1545 purge.

I have spent ten years
Building a grass hut;
Now winds occupy half,
The moon fills the rest.
Alas, I cannot let you come in,
But I shall receive you outside.

———————

I discuss with my heart
Whether to retire from court.

My heart scorns the intent:
"How could you leave the king?"
"Heart, stay here and serve Him,
My old body must go."

Do not grieve, little birds,
Over the falling blossoms:
They're not to blame, it's the wind
Who loosens and scatters the petals.
Spring is leaving us.
Don't hold it against her.

Yi Hwang
[1501–1571]

Perhaps the most famous Neo-Confucianist in Korea, called "the Sage of the East," who served as Minister of Rites during the time of King Sŏnjo. Among other works, his commentaries on the philosophy of Chu Hsi are well known. When he was living in a hermitage among the mountains, he wrote a *sijo* cycle, *Twelve Songs of Mt. To* (1565), which praised, and moralized upon, the beauties of the mountain.

Even a foolish fellow can know and act.
Is it not easy, learning the Way?
Even a sage cannot know all and act.
Is it not difficult, learning the Way?
While I study and work, easy or difficult,
I do not see old age creeping upon me.

Only I and the seagull
Know the thirty-six peaks of Mt. Ch'ŏngnyang.
Seagulls might report Arcadia is here;
Even more untrustworthy are peach blossoms.
O blossoms, do not fall, do not float down
To tell the fisherman of this sunny site.

It is true that men of old
Did not see me nor I them.
No, I cannot see them: but
Before us lies their virtuous way.
Since we have the Way, the Progress,
What else is there to do but follow?

Cho Sik
[1501–1572]

He was a good scholar, but never took office, and lived as a hermit on Mt. Turyu. Although summons came many times from the government, he always excused himself. An anthology records two poems of his; this one was written to express his sorrow over the death of King Myŏngjong.

Wearing cotton clothes in the coldest winter,
Wet with rain and snow in the wild,
I have not had the sun,
Hidden by the clouds, among these caves.
But, yet, to see the setting sun
Brings out my longing for its light.

Kim In-hu
[1510–1560]

A great scholar and a friend of Yi Hwang, who, after the death of King Injong (1545), retired from court and lived a solitary life.

The great pine we felled yesterday
With its high long branches—
Had we left it longer, it would
Have yielded beams, lesser and greater.
When the Royal Hall declines, alas,
What tree will serve to uphold the state?

Hongnang

A famous *kisaeng* and dancer during the reign of King Sŏnjo (1552–1568–1608). She was born in Hongwŏn, South Hamgyŏng Province. In the autumn of 1573 she accompanied Ch'oe Kyŏng-ch'ang (1539–1583), a noted poet of the day, on his official mission to the north. When, in 1574, Ch'oe had to return to the capital, she sent him the following poem of farewell.

> I send you branches of the willow—
> Plant them, my Lord, to be admired,
> Outside your bedroom window.
> Perhaps the night rain will make them bud:
> Think, then, that it is I
> Who have come to be with you.

Ch'ŏn Kŭm

Another famous *kisaeng*; nothing is known of her life.

> Night draws near in a dead village,
> A dog barks far away.
> I open the cottage door:
> The chilly sky and the moon.
> Be still, stop barking at the moon
> Asleep over the bare mountain.

Myŏngok

> They say dream visits
> are "only a dream."
> My longing to see him
> is destroying me.

Where else
do I see him but in dreams?
Darling, come to me
even if it be in dreams:
let me see you, let me
see you time and time again.

Song In
[1517–1584]

He married the third daughter of King Chungjong, Princess Chŏng-sun, and was enfeoffed as the Lord of Yŏsŏng. He associated with Yi Hwang and Yi I, famous scholars of the day.

Forget at once what you have heard,
Overlook at once what you have seen.
Since I live according to this rule,
I, meddle with others? Never.
Only my hands work, they are ready:
They know how to exchange cups.

Yang Sa-ŏn
[1517–1584]

He was governor of many towns in the neighborhood of the Diamond Mountains and therefore privileged to frequent those beauty spots, where he composed the following poem.

However high a mountain may be,
It still is lower than the sky.
Climb, climb again, and higher, who says
You will not gain the summit?
People complain it is too high,
With no trial, no attempt, no will.

Yu Hŭi-ch'un
[d. 1577]

Yu passed the final civil service examination in 1538 and, after a distinguished official career, retired to his native village in 1575.

> I offer you a bundle of parsley,
> Fresh, clean.
> A bundle of parsley just for you,
> No one else, God forbid, just you.
> Maybe not too delicious, my Dear,
> But try again; once more test and taste.

Kwŏn Ho-mun
[1532–1587]

He was a disciple of Yi Hwang, but did not take office, and lived below Mt. Ch'ŏngsŏng all his life.

> Serve the King, do good to the people,
> Fish by moonlight, plow among the clouds—
> A wise gentleman
> Enjoys life in this way.
> Wealth and rank are dangerous games.
> I will live, yes, live poor and humble.

> Nature makes clear the windy air,
> Bright the round moon.
> In the bamboo garden and on the
> Pine fence not a speck of dust.
> How fresh and fervent my life
> With a long lute and piled scrolls!

83

Sŏng Hon
[1535–1598]

Owing to illness he did not take the civil service examination. A man of wide learning, he refused to take office and taught his disciples at Ugye, a village northwest of Seoul. Of his philosophical writings the most famous was a series of correspondence with Yi I on Neo-Confucian metaphysics. King Injo honored him with the posthumous title of Second State Counselor. His *Collected Works* were first published in 1682, a second edition was published in 1809.

> The mountain is silent,
> The water without form.
> A clear breeze has no price,
> The bright moon no owner.
> Here, after their fashion,
> I will grow old in peace.

Yi I
[1536–1584]

Together with Yi Hwang, Yi I is perhaps one of the most celebrated Neo-Confucianists in Korea. An infant prodigy, he knew Chinese script at the age of three, and when he was seven he already composed poems in Chinese. At the age of nineteen he entered the Diamond Mountains and was initiated in Buddhism, but soon abandoned it for the study of the philosophy of Chu Hsi. After serving as Minister of Personnel and War, and Rector of the National Academy, he returned to Haeju in 1576, had a house built on Mt. Ko, and taught disciples there. The nine scenes of which he sings in the following poems are to be found in the Suyang Mountain in Haeju. The first poem is a prologue; the rest of the nine poems cover the four seasons of the year. The nine place names are used as imagery for poetic amplification. In the first poem, for example, a place name "Kwanam" is at the same time an image, "the crown rock."

84

NINE SONGS OF MT. KO

Waters of Mt. Ko and their nine scenes,
They are not yet known to men.
But I weed and weave a grass hut there
And my friends come in two's and three's.
I would fancy I am on Mt. Wu-i,[1]
And follow the steps of Master Chu.[2]

Where shall we find the first song?
The sun lances the crown rock, and
Mist clears above the tall grass.
Lo the magic views far and near—
Calling my friends I would wait
With a green goblet in the pine grove.

We shall intone the second song
By the brocaded rock in late spring.
There let the green waves bear away
The blossoms to the distant fields.
Can the dusty world fathom this joy?
I must tell men of this sunny place.

We shall hum our third song
Where leaves paint screens of jade.
Birds alight by the green water,
Sylvan friends drum and twitter.
Twisted pines brave a clear breeze,
And lament summer's brief glory.

When the sun crosses the pine cliff,
Let us sing our fourth song.
Rocks swim in the water's bosom,
They weave a rainbow of another sky.
Trees and springs are deep and good; my heart
Dances with an exalted joy.

Shall we sing our fifth song
By the screens, solemn and secret?

My humble study by the water,
O how remote, cool and free.
Here I will work to my heart's content, and make
Poems of moon and breeze.

We find the sixth song by the gorge
Where waters gurgle over silver scales.
There I and fishes delight:
Who else has a larger heart?
At twilight I walk homeward,
A rod on my shoulder and the moon above.

We sing our seventh song by the rock,
Where the scarlet leaves are autumn queens.
Traceries of frost curtain the rocks—
See the brocade on the hanging cliffs.
Alone I sit on the cold stone,
I forget to return home.

We shall hear our eighth song
When moon blesses the tinkling brook.
There I will play, play on the lute,
With jade plectrums and a gold bridge.
New tunes cannot compare with the old,
But I am happy—I am alone.

When the winter crosses Mt. Mun,
There we shall sing our ninth song.
Snow falls thick and covers over
The rugged rocks and the strange stones.
Nobody comes here for pleasure now,
Fools say there is nothing to see.

Chŏng Ch'ŏl
[1537–1594]

Poet, politician, and musician, Chŏng became a *chinsa* in 1561. He had a turbulent political career and became Second State Counselor in the reign of King Sŏnjo. His life was thorny due to party strife, and he had to suffer many exiles. He died on Kanghwa Island on February 7, 1594. The *Pine River Anthology*, a collection of his *kasa* and *sijo*, contains seventy-four shorter poems and five long poems. He was subtle in weaving words together and relied for effect on a cunning juxtaposition which "gave back a familiar word as new."

The juice of bitter herbs
Has more taste than any meat.
My snail-shell hut of grass
Is a fitting abode for me.
But my love for the King persists;
It chokes me and tears my heart.

Whether or not I live on bran and chaff,
Whether or not I have a single gourd cup,
Or even if my family be in great disorder,
I will live on
With confidence
If my King chooses to love me.

Were I to spread my wings here
And flap them twice or thrice,
I could see my beloved lord
On the first peak of Mt. Pongnae.
But what good is it to prate
And run my head against the wall?

I'd like to break up this body,
Let its pieces float on the blue.

If that water would sob and flow down
To the rapids of the Han River,
Only then could I cure my disease
Of yearning for my beloved lord.

———————

Snow falls on the pine grove;
Trees blossom.
I wish I could break a branch
And send it to my King.
No matter if the blossoms fade
After he has seen my branch.

———————

In the slanting evening sun
Sky and river are a single color.
O cackling geese, flying among
The burning maples and feathery reeds.
Autumn is almost gone;
Why does he still keep silent?

———————

Rise and fall—fortune's rhythm.
Thick grows the autumn grass in Taebang.
Let the shepherd's careless pipe
Hymn events now long forgotten.
How about trying a cup, my friend,
In this peaceful and happy age?

———————

Yesterday they told me the wine was ripe
In Mr. Sŏng's [1] house over the hill.
So I kick up a sleeping ox,
Put on a saddlecloth and mount.
"Boy, is your master at home?
Tell him, his friend Chŏng is here."

———————

Mr. Ko [2] builds a grass hut
Somewhere on the South Mountain.

88

His tenants are flowers and the moon,
As well as stones and water.
He must keep wine also;
He invites me for a cup.

Would I envy others' laughter,
Discarding the anguish of my heart?
Would I join in another's party,
Discarding a cup of my own wine?
Would my first love be forgotten,
My burning heart fresh as jade?

I have idled my time away;
Roved aimlessly here and there.
My words and deeds lack sincerity;
I have achieved nothing.
It's all over, it's all over;
Why not enjoy the rest of my life?

Let's strain sour wine and drink
Until our mouths become sour,
Let's steam bitter herbs and chew
Until they become sweet.
Let's walk up and down the street
Until the nails in our clogs have worn flat.

After ten years I admire again
The white jade cup in the Hongmun Hall.[3]
Its limpid color
Has not changed as time passed.
But why does the mind of man
Play us false morning and night?

How could you leave it to rot,
The lumber fit for beams and rafters?

Small men indulge in hot debate
In the torn and tumble-down house.
O carpenters with ink cup and measure,
You rush about to no purpose.

The classic tower soars higher,
After eight centuries of Silla glory.
The boom of the gigantic bell,
O how clear at each stroke.
The crystal sound crosses the field,
Quickens the dusk in a desolate arbor.

A dash of rain upon the delicate
Lotus leaves. But the leaves
Remain unmarked, no matter
How hard the raindrops beat.
Mind, be like the lotus leaves,
Unstained by the mad world.

Let forty thousand pecks of pearls
Rest on the lotus leaves.
I box them and measure them
To send them off to the passing winds.
Tumultuous rolling drops—
How abundant, how graceful.

Last night over Wu-ling [4] hills
Under threatening clouds
A pair of phoenix showed themselves, and dallied
In amorous pursuit of one another.
They dropped a feather here and there;
But don't look to find them on this earth.

Look, a shadow on the stream—
A monk crosses the bridge.

Stop awhile, cowled traveler,
Where does your journey take you?
He does not turn around but walks on,
Pointing to the white clouds with his stick.

Boys have gone out to gather bracken;
The pine grove is bare of guests.
Who will pick up the dice
Scattered on the checkerboard?
Drunk, I lean on the pine trunk,
Let dusk and dawn pass me by.

You wheel around, noble bird,
Until you shed your white feathers.
And soaring high in the blue vault,
You speak:
"I shall soar and soar again
Until I have glimpsed the cosmos."

Milky rain on the green hills,
Can you deceive me?
A sedge cape and horsehair hat,
Can you deceive me?
Yesterday I flung off my silk robe—
I have nothing that will stain me.

The fourth string on the Black Lute
Softens and soothes my spirit.
I pluck the gallant note,
Play a pizzicato with vigor.
Don't feel sad, somber string,
I shall return and pluck you shortly.

I pluck the second note on the fourth string
Of the Lute of the Black Crane.

The sound surges like a stream broken forth from the ice,
Rushing toward the sea.
Distant raindrops, too, play in concert;
They beat lightly on the lotus leaves.

I meet my old love after years,
Fall in love with her over again.
Her airs and graces of long ago
Haunt me afresh.
Love, if my mind had been changed,
I could have looked away when you came.

I know autumn has come—
The paulownia has shed its leaves.
Cool, cool is the night,
A silk rain falls on the clear river.
My love is a thousand miles away;
I cannot sleep.

I bade you farewell, my love,
When fallen leaves danced in the wind.
Now snow and ice have melted,
Blossoms will soon adorn the day.
But you send me no word—
Alas, my love, no word.

Flowers are in splendid show,
Butterflies fly in pairs.
Willows are green, luxuriant,
Orioles sing in pairs.
Birds and beasts are loving, always two together—
But why do I dwell here alone?

THE WANDERINGS
1580

Among rivers and lakes I lay sick
Lying among bamboo groves I rested.
Then the King summoned me, made me Governor;
I leave for my new post, eight hundred leagues away.
O royal favor, imperishable grace.
I enter the Yŏnch'u Gate, bow toward the South Gate,
bid farewell to my Lord and withdraw,
and find a man holding a jade tally.[1]
I change horses at P'yŏnggu Station and follow the Yŏ.
Where is Sŏm River? Mount Ch'i is here.
O waters of Soyang,[2] whither do you flow?
When a lonely subject leaves the court,
nothing happens except that he gets old.

After a sleepless night at Ch'ŏrwŏn,
I climb up to Pukkwan Arbor,
scanning the first peak of Mount Samgak.
Magpies at the site of T'aebong,[3]
do you know the rise and fall of changing ages?
I dream of Chi Ch'ang-ju,[4] his noble figure,
his love of people, his good government.
O Hoeyang of my town, Huai-yang of the Former Han.

My hostel is quiet—it is March.
A path along Hwach'on stretches to the Diamond Mountains.
I fling off coat and sack and mend a stone path;
I let my staff lead me on from ravine to ravine.
From Paekch'ŏn Canyon I enter Manp'ok Grotto.
There, silver rainbows, dragons with jade tails;
turning and coiling, tail biting tail,
they spurt cataracts, rend the hills.
Listen, it is thunder; look, it is snow.

On the top of the sheer Kŭmgang precipice,
home of black-and-gray cranes,
woken by spring breeze and jade flute

the noble birds in white and gray silk
beat the air and chariot the clouds
to greet Lin Pu,[5] master of the West Lake.
Looking downward, the chasms and hollows are censers,
I am at the Chŏngyang Temple on the Chinhyŏl Terrace.
O face of Mount Lu,[6] immortal landscape!
Extravagant and festive Creator! What abundance of strange forms!
He has made these fantastic peaks as easily
as if he were planting lotus; in the ravines
he seems to have gathered up all the jade in the world—
nothing to him to kick the ocean out of the way
and spin the North Pole in his hand!
Lofty Manggo Terrace and lonely Hyŏlmang Peak
stand high and praise their Maker,
Constant and unbending for millions of years.
Can we match your steadfastness?

From the Kaesim Terrace I view the Chunghyang Castle
and count twelve thousand peaks in the clear air.
If we could gather the essence of air's vitality,
if we could bottle the noble soul of the mountains,
and bring them back to create a Man—
ah, what a man that would be!
O multiple figures, baffling shapes,
made in eternity by the Lord of All—O joy,
I see them with dazzled eyes.

Who has ever stood on the Piro Peak?
Which is higher, Mount Tung or Mount T'ai? [7]
Who said the kingdom of Lu was small?
Who said all under Heaven appeared to him small?
One does not know the limit of his thought;
better descend, if you cannot gain the summit.[8]

After Wŏnt'ong Cave I pick a path,
reach Lion Peak and gaze from a giant rock.
A bearded dragon in the Fiery Dragon Lake
floats day and night and reaches the ocean.
When will you reach the wind and the clouds?

When will you send the sweet rain
to the yellowing leaves on a cracked cliff?
Seeing Magayŏn, Maitreya on a cliff,[9] and Anmun Hill,
I cross a decaying wooden bridge to a terrace, a cliff
hanging in air, a thousand fathoms deep.
The Milky Way unfastens its whole spool of thread,
hung like the warp and woof of a cloth.
Twelve cascades in nature's map: O wonder.
Had Li Po been here and mulled over again,
he would have been ashamed of Lu Cataract.[10]

Let us leave the mountain and go to the sea.
A bamboo sedan chair descends by the Sanyŏng Pavilion.
The birds and the lucid torrent hate to part.
Unfurl a banner, five colors brave the sky,
beat the drum and play on the flute, music
rolls away clouds and seas.
Hoofs carry the drunken poet onto the sand;
soon I am in the midst of sea plants.
Gulls fly back and forth to greet me.

After Kŭmnan Cave I climb to Ch'ongsŏk Arbor and see
four pillars of the palace of the fairies,
work of a masterful artisan of ancient China,
touch of dexterous ax, supreme craft.
What is meant by its six-sided shape?

Leaving Kosŏng behind, I reach the Three-Days-Bank.[11]
The six red letters are still on the cliff—but
where are the four noble knights of Silla?
After their three days here, where did they go?
To Sŏnyu Ravine or to Yŏngnang Lake?
To the Ch'ŏnggan Arbor or Man'gyŏng Terrace?

Peach blossoms scatter, a cuckoo calls.
I rise at midnight on the Ŭisang Terrace to await
the rising sun. Lucky clouds appear,
thick on the horizon; six dragons
uphold and push: the sun climbs.

The whole world shakes in its light,
it shines in mid-air, I can count its hair.
May the clouds never cover its shining.
Yes Li Po is dead, but his poems endure.
How subtly he sang of this magnificence.

Lightly treading the azaleas on Mount Hyŏn,
the noble carriage rolls down to Kyŏngp'o in the sunset.
Behind the fierce pines on the stretched silk
the sea is calm, clear as the pebbles are numerous.
I row a boat and pass under Kangmun Bridge.
Here the ocean is forever placid,
broad and fair, liberal in temper.
People still tell the tale of Hongjang,[12]
that ravishing woman, her bewitching charm.
Kangnŭng Province, famed for virtue and good customs—
Flagpoles for filial sons adorn the valleys.
Truly the people of Yao and Shun linger here still.

The Osip flows below Pearl House and Chuksŏ Pavilion,
catching the green of the T'aebaek Mountains.
Could I make it flow to the Han below Mount South?
Journeys have limits, but landscapes are infinite.
My heart is full; I will brave the wanderer's sorrow—[13]
To fathom the depths of clouds and seas
the poet asks, standing at Mangyang Arbor:
"Heaven lies beyond seas; what is beyond heaven?"
Did I enrage the furious whale? It blows,
it bellows and roars! The silver mountain
is leveled, it crashes, breaks. Snow in the May sky.

Night falls and winds and waves lull.
I wait for the moon from the sea.
The lucky moon plays between clouds and waves,
with a lance of light a thousand feet long.
I roll up a pearl screen and sweep
the jade stairs. While I await a daystar,
someone sends me a spray of white lotus.
O let this world be revealed to all!

Brimming a cup with enchanted wine
I question the moon: "Where are the heroes,
where are the four knights of yesteryear?"
No one listens; I am not answered.
Yes, I have miles to go in this magic land.

I doze to sleep, leaning my head on the pine trunk.
A voice whispers to me in my dream:
You are a benign faery from Elysium
who misread the word in the Yellow Book,[14]
banished from heaven to the world of men.
But linger on, friend, taste my immortal wine.
Pouring from the Big Dipper, filling from the Ocean,
he himself drinks and offers me a cup.
One cup, two cups, we drink by turns until
the warm breeze lifts me by the arm
and I stride into the great void.
Let us divide this wine among the four seas.
Let the whole world drink and be in wine.
Then let us meet again and exchange cups.
Words spoken, he soared skyward on a crane's back.
Only a flute rings in the void. When was it?
Awakened I look downward. I know not its depth
nor its breadth; I mean the sea.
Only the moonlight shining everywhere.[15]

HYMN OF CONSTANCY
c. 1585–1587

I was born to serve you
by happy affinity, Heaven's wish.
My youth was spent for you; you loved
me alone. What can match
this undivided mind, this rare love?
I wanted to spend my whole life with you.
Why do we live apart in our later age?
Once I repaired with you to the Moon Palace;
but then I was left here below. Three years now
since my hair became disheveled, unkempt.

For whom should I dress myself?
My mind, tied in knots of anxiety,
grief, piled fold upon fold,
only produces sighs, only tears.
Life has an end; sorrow is endless.

Fickle time flows, flows forever, and cold and heat
come and go, as if they know time.
Much to hear and see, much to feel every season.
Spring winds hollow out snow and stir the plum trees;
O fragrance in the cool of the air. And then,
the moonlight at dusk, kindly and welcoming,
plays over my pillow. Is it my Lord, is it not?
Were I to send him a plum branch,
what would he think when he saw it?

Flowers are gone, a green shade adorns the ground.
Gauze and embroidered curtains are drawn in vain.
A lotus curtain pulled aside, I set a peacock screen.
But what good is it, a long cruel day?
Cut the silk stuff with Mandarin-duck designs,
loosen the thread of five different colors,
and measure it off with a golden measure:
I make his clothes deftly and with style.
On a coral carrier, in a jade box, I offer him
this garment, gazing toward his far abode—
Mountains are rugged, clouds are ominous,
Who will risk these thousand miles?
Would he welcome me if I went?

When frost falls and wild geese flutter overhead,
When I stand on the tower rolling up the crystal screen,
the moon rises, and stars glitter in the north—
is that he? I rush out to meet him:
Nothing. But tears blind my eyes.
Let me send you a handful of sunrays—
please, hang them on your tower, let them shine
over eight corners and make every hill and valley
bright, bright as the day.

Now snow has covered and frozen the whole world;
both men and birds are vanished from sight.
And when this place is cold as it is now,
how cold must he be in that high pavilion!
Would I might capture spring, make it shine on him;
would I might offer him the sunlight
that once shone on the eaves of my cottage.
Tucking up my red skirt, rolling
my blue sleeves, I take a long stick
and wander out in the sunset.
A thousand thoughts are too many.
The day was short; but at night I sit up
with a mica-inlaid lute by the blue lamp,
my chin in my hand, hoping to dream of him.
O cold is the quilt, long is the night.

Twelve times a day, thirty days in the month,
in vain I try to bury this grief
that masters me and pierces me to the marrow.
Not even ten doctors can cure my sickness.
This is all, alas, all due to my Lord.
Better to die and become a butterfly,
stop at each flower, rest upon branches
with scented wings,
and die again upon his cloak.
He may not remember me: yet I will follow him.

THE DIALOGUE OF TWO COURT LADIES
c. 1585–1587

"Lady, whose face I know, lady
walking alone, tell me,
why did you leave the royal palace,
whom are you seeking as the sun goes down?"
"Hear then my story.
                    My face and ways
do not deserve his royal love, I know;

yet when he sees, he deigns to recognize me . . .
welcomes me as of old.
I cannot believe him changed.
I lie and think, sit and measure,
my sins heap up like mountains.
I do not quarrel with heaven or with men.
Untie this sadness, undo this sorrow?
No, it seems it is my ordained fate."

"Don't fret, my dear. There's something
eating *his* heart out, too.
I've served him, I know him.

                     He has had
little enough of peace these days, God knows.
Spring cold and summer heat,
long autumn and rueful winter days,
how did he spend them? Who served him?
Morning gruel and daily rice,
did he get enough?
Has he slept well, think you,
these long nights?"

"Ah, I want his news—but day is gone.
Would someone come tomorrow—restless thought!
Where shall I go, led or pushed?

                     The clouds
gather on solemn peaks, a mist
bewraps the world.

                How then, lady,
can I see the brightness,
the brightness of sun and moon?
What's there—within a foot, within an inch?
A thousand miles is far, so far. . . . I'll go
down to the sea and wait a boat.
O, winds and waves are furious—I'm stunned—
the boatman's gone—only the empty ship. . . .

Now darkness
creeps under the eaves of a hut. For whom
does that lamp burn on the wall there?
Up hill and down I go, or pace the shore.
At last my prayer is answered, and I see
Milord in dreams.
                    But time
has stolen away his jade face.
                         I want
to tell him all, all, to my heart's content,
but tears choke me, words stick in my throat.
I cannot speak my love or melt my grief.
A frivolous cock crows. Everything
was a mocking dream.
I open the window; only the shadows hover.
O, to be the moon and shine on his window."

"Lady, the moon, say you?
Rather a weeping rain!"

LITTLE ODES OF MOUNT STAR
c. 1585–1587

An unknown guest in passing
stopped on Mount Star and said:
"Listen, Master of the Sŏha Hall,[1]
despite the many pleasures life held,
why did you prefer to them all
this mountain, this water?
What made you choose
the solitude of hills and streams?"

1

Sweeping away the pine needles,
setting a cushion on a bamboo couch
I casually climb into the seat
and view the Four Corners.

Floating clouds come and go
over the Sŏsŏk Terrace;
their flying motion and gentle gestures
resemble the mind and courtesy
of the noble Master of Sŏha.
The fresh stream, gold and silver,
flows past the Arbor;
as if the Weaver Star [2] had come to earth
the water rushes in endless patterns,
like pink dawn clouds, scissored and spread before us.
In the city, without a calendar who would know
the year's cycle? But here
every subtle change of the seasons
unrolls like a screen before us.
This is truly the land of the Immortals.

2

Sun at the window caresses the plum tree;
the fragrance of blossoms wakes me.
Who says there is nothing
to keep an old hermit busy?
I sow melons, tend them, support them;
when the rain nurtures the young plants,
I think of the old tale of the Blue Gate.[3]
In straw sandals, with a bamboo cane,
I follow the peach-snowed causeway
over to Pangch'o Islet.
As I stroll by the West Brook
the stone screen accompanies me
in the water mirror, painted there, as if polished.
Where is Arcadia? Peach Blossom Spring is here.

3

The casual south wind
disperses the tree shade, makes way
for a faithful cuckoo—where has he flown from?
I wake from a doze

on the pillow of ancient worthies
and see the reflected balcony floating
among the clouds in the lake.
With my arrowroot hat aslant
and my smock tucked into my belt,
I go nearer, and watch the drunken fishes
after the rainy night.
Here and there, red and white lotus:
their fragrance rises
into the windless sky
and passes over the hills.
As though I had met with Chou Tun-yi [4] and supped
on the Ultimate Secret—
or as if a faery had shown me the Jade Letters [5]—
I glance toward Noja Rock by Chami shore,
letting a tall pine screen the sun,
sitting at ease on the stone path.

4

In the bitter world of man it is June;
here in Elysium the air has the feel
of autumn.
A duck afloat on the stream moves in
to the white sand bar,
makes friends with the gulls.
Free and leisurely, it resembles
our host, the noble Master of Sŏha.

5

At the fourth watch the moon rises,
cold, over the paulownia trees.
Thousand cliffs, ten thousand ravines—
could they be brighter by daylight?
Who moved the Palace of Crystal from Huchou? [6]
Did I cross the Milky Way?
Have I reached the Moon Palace?

Setting out from the twin pines,
I let the boat drift downstream
passing the floating duckweed, pink and white.
My friend, when did we reach
the cataract below Hwanbyŏk Hall?
Cowherds in the riverside pastures
were joyfully playing their pipes in the sunset light.
Do not awaken the sleeping dragon,
do not let cranes abandon their nests and take wing
into the smoky mid-air.
Su Shih in his poem on Red Cliff [7]
praises the seventh moon above all;
but let us not underestimate
the August moon.
When the clouds part and water grows still,
the rising moon anchors herself in a pine branch.
They say Li Po drowned because of her.

6

North winds sweep away
the heaped leaves on the wild mountains,
marshal the clouds, attack us with snow.
The Creator, He who loves
to fashion the things of nature,
makes snowflowers of white jade, devises
myriad new forms for the forests.
The foreshore freezes over.
Over the one-logged bridge
goes an old monk, a stick on his shoulder.
Where do you head for, friend? What temple
is richer in beauty than what you see
here in this world of the moon,
Mount Star in a fresh snowfall?

7

Alone in the deep mountain
with no friend but the classics, pile on pile,

I think of the men of all times:
many were sages, many were heroes.
Heavenly intention goes into the making of men.
Yet fortunes rise and fall, and what is unknowable
seems to be chance. And sadness is deep.
Why did Hsü Yu on Mount Chi
cleanse his innocent ears? [8]

8

The mind of the Master of Sŏha Hall
smiles like his face;
his friendship is new and fresh each day.
Let us not think of worldly affairs.
The wine brewed yesterday must be ready:
Let's drink, passing the cup back and forth,
pouring more wine till we are tired of it.
Then our hearts will be open, the net
of sorrow unraveled to nothing.
String the black lute and pluck "Wind in the Pines,"
Who is host, who is guest?
The flying crane is the true Immortal
I met once in the Moon Palace.
The guest addresses the host with a word:
"You, sir, you alone are immortal."

A TIME TO DRINK

Let us drink a cup, and then another,
After drinking let us pluck a flower,
Let the flowers lie as we drink more.
When your body dies, it will be wrapped
In a mat and dragged along by a rope,
Or else, with last rites and painted carriages,
A thousand friends will follow you in tears.
And when you are laid away among the bracken,
Under tawny oaks and shivering poplars,
When the yellow sun shines and the moon rises,

And when a fine rain or thick snow falls,
And when the chilly winds mourn there,
Who, who will offer you a cup of wine?
Furthermore, when only a monkey whistles,
What good will it do you to regret, my dear,
The wine you forbore to drink while you were alive?

Yi Sun-sin
[1545–1598]

The most famous Korean admiral, whose services turned the tide of
war during the Japanese invasion (1592–1598). A genius in naval tac-
tics, he invented a highly effective warship of his own, the turtle boat,
first ironclad warship in history. It was shaped like a tortoise and could
fire flaming arrows into the thick of the enemy ships, and thereby won
every sea battle. The admiral was also a gifted poet.

> On the garrison tower,
> In the moonlit Hansan Isle,
> A great sword beside me,
> I sit alone, sunk in sorrow.
> Listen, a reed-leaf whistle in the dark—
> It pierces my entrails; aye, they shake.

Yi Wŏn-ik
[1547–1634]

He rendered distinguished services during the Japanese invasion and
recaptured P'yŏngyang from the enemy. He was later Chief State
Counselor under Kwanghaegun. This is his only surviving poem.

> What if the willow has ten thousand strings;
> Can they tie down the spring breeze?
> What if the bees and butterflies search out nectar;

Can they stop the falling blossoms?
What if we feel secure in the time of our love;
What will become of it if she leaves me alone?

Im Che
[1549–1587]

Born in Naju, he was a man of unmatched genius and phenomenal memory; he was supposed to have memorized a thousand words of verse a day. His reputation was unparalleled during his lifetime, and his contemporaries, including such a great scholar-poet as Yi I, praised him as "a remarkable man." Of passionate and sensuous nature, the thirty-six years of his life were filled with trouble. Having heard of the fame of Hwang Chin-i, he made a poetic pilgrimage to Songdo. But when he called at her house, he learned that she was already dead. Distressed and unable to suppress his sorrow, he visited her tomb and composed and recited this tribute to her memory:

> On the hill where the grass grows long,
> Are you sleeping, or lying at rest?
> Only bones are here,
> Your once beautiful face, where is it,
> My darling, where did it go? Alas,
> To whom should I offer this cup?

Cho Chon-sŏng
[1553–1627]

He came of an important scholar's family in Yangju and became a subprefect at the age of twenty, and later, Governor of Kangwŏn Province. He also fought during the Japanese invasion. Four poems survive, all addressed to a boy. He was a poet of individual simplicity, and tenderness of feeling and expression grace his poems.

> Boy, fetch your open basket,
> The sun is setting.

The ferns which grew last night
Are already withered, I fear.
What is the poor man's daily food,
But the fiddlehead guileless and pure?

Boy, put on a sedge cape and bamboo hat;
It rains by the eastern torrent.
With a long rod and no hook,
Let's go angling in the rain.
Quiet there, fish, don't be startled!
I came here elated, in high spirits.

Boy, lead a cow to the northern village,
Let's taste the new-made wine.
Having drained to the lees, I'll return home
On cow-back under the moon.
Hurrah, I am a Fu Hsi tonight,
The ancient glories are at my fingertips.

Ch'a Ch'ŏn-no
[1556–1615]

He passed a special examination which was held in the National Academy on the occasion of the royal visit to the Confucian Temple (1577). He excelled in verse and prose in Chinese, and his works were characterized by rich texture and pungent wit. During the Japanese invasion, when armies of Ming China came to Korea's aid, Ch'a and other leading men of letters were called upon to draw up documents, correspondence, and manifestoes. Upon the withdrawal of the Ming Army, King Sŏnjo ordered five writers to compose farewell verses, and Ch'a is said to have produced 600 stanzas overnight.

THE COUNTRY LIFE

To exercise my talent or leave my mark,
That is not my intention, not at all.

What is a name? What is a rank?
I would rather view Mt. Shang [1] and follow
The way of the four bearded sages.
Riches are not for me.
Among mountains and rivers,
Among the ravines and pine woods, I build
A grass-roofed hut with a brushwood door.
Among turnips and blue
Creeping plants, under a misty moon,
In this dense forest where clouds nest,
Among pine trees where only dogs bark,
Who would find this snowy site?
I sing of a hedge made of pine branches
And of fungus with purplish stalk.
I sow and plow with the spring rain. [2]
Not for me a carriage with four horses;
I find pleasure in the hills and waters.
Only the virtuous are truly wise.
Today I climb the hill and whistle long;
Tomorrow I go to a stream and compose.
With coarse clothes, with a bamboo stick,
I go to the mountain torrent and there
While away my time among the pines.
The fiddlehead fern is my breakfast;
The fish I caught will do for a supper.
After a few poems I row my boat,
Drop a line into the twilight river.
How could this old fisherman know
The nine highways and that life of care?
And who in the muddy world would know
My joy in drifting on the green waves?
Silver scales ripple, jade bodies dart
Where the water and sky are a single color.
I catch a big-mouthed, fine-scaled fish
That surpasses a perch of the Pine River.
Having hung a rod on the reed awning,
I beach my boat on a long sand spit

In the smoky twilight; gulls fly back and forth.
Or I tie my boat by the twilit riverbank;
My sandals ramble toward a mountain village.
Look, on the hills to the north and south,
Several roofs swim in the blue smoke.
Thus with a lute and books a day passes.
Now let us draw the wine from the cask,
Exchange a cup with songs and ballads.
Having drained to the lees, you know what I mean,
Let's take a stone for a pillow, fall into a doze.
Only at the whoop of a crane will we wake
With the lucid moon mirrored in the blue.
Above all, I endorse a calm and simple life. . . .
Thus will I live, and live ten thousand years.

Yi Tŏk-hyŏng
[1561–1613]

Born in Kyŏngju, he was dispatched to Ming China during the Japanese invasion and succeeded in securing a military alliance. Together with the Chinese soldiers, his army retook P'yŏngyang and attacked the enemy at Ulsan. He befriended Pak In-no, master of the kasa form, and two poems survive.

The moon hung in the sky, bright, full.
Since the dawn,
It has met wind and frost.
Alas, soon it will sink.
But no, wait, I say,
And shine on the gold cup of a drunken guest.

Kim Sang-yong
[1561–1637]

Born in Andong, he became a chinsa in 1582 and served as Third State Counselor under King Injo (1595–1623–1649). When Kanghwa

Island fell into the hands of the Manchu. he climbed on the South Gate of the fortress and died with tragic bravery by blowing himself to pieces with gunpowder.

> Love is a deceit—
> She does not love me.
> She says
> She comes to me in dream:
> It is a lie.
> All night awake and restless,
> Where shall I see her, in what dream?

> Fierce beats the rain
> On the paulownia's wide
> Majestic leaves.
> My grief awakes and twists my heart,
> The loud rain beats on my sorrow.
> Never again shall I plant
> A tree with such broad leaves.

Pak In-no
[1561–1643]

Author of sixty-eight *sijo* and seven *kasa* poems, he rendered conspicuous service during the Japanese invasion. In 1599 he passed the military service examination and served as commander of a strategic island off the Korean coast. In 1605, however, his military career ended, and he turned his talents to a study of the classics and living a carefree hermit life. In 1611 Yi Tŏk-hyŏng came to the South to escape from unsavory conditions at court. Pak was on drinking terms with Yi, for whom he wrote the "Song of the Sedge Bank" (1611) which praises Yi's idle life and elegant pleasure at Saje ("Sedge Bank"). Asked by Yi about his life in the mountains, Pak wrote the following *kasa*, which asserts the joy and contentment of a life of poverty and declares that the virtue of a gentleman is "to be poor and yet not resent" his poverty.

111

IN PRAISE OF POVERTY
c. 1611–1613

Foolish and impractical I am, no man is more so.
I trust to luck, and deep in this rustic corner
Build myself a grass hut, cook rice or make gruel
In the windy morning and the rainy evening,
With straws wet from wind and rain.
But why so much smoke, volumes of smoke?
I offer my empty stomach only lukewarm rice tea.

Although my days are spent in this manner,
Will a man of spirit yield his will?
Poor but untarnished, aim high, live honest.
O contradiction, O necessity.
If autumn is short, let spring be plentiful.
If pocket is empty, let the bottle be filled.
Penury harasses more than one man.

Let hunger and cold threaten my living warmth,
Sincerity's bright red burns in me still.
Imbued with public spirit, forgetting myself,
With knapsacks, with bags, I took to the field [1]
To die in the last ditch; I fought
My country's battle for five years, stepped over
Bodies that lay in heaps, forded a river of blood.
So my days went by: my house was empty.

An old, long-bearded servant forgets
The status of master and servant.
Who will inform me of the nearing spring?
Whom should I ask to plow the field?
An old man farms there, sows and reaps.
He is I, an old man in rustic winds.
Look at him among the asarum plants,
Look at him bending over a distant mound.
No one will say he is mean; but
However much I intend to plow,
Can I do it without an ox?

112

Crops are backward this year after the long drought,
But to the westward land I bring water from a puddle,
And wend a moonless path at dusk to one
Who has half promised to lend me an ox.
Standing outside the firmly closed door, I cough
Loudly, twice or thrice.
"Who's there?" "Shameless me."
"What has brought you here at night?"
"It is improper to come every year, I know;
But I am here for an ox."
"I would certainly let you use it;
But last night my neighbor invited me
For a red pheasant cooked on a charcoal fire,
Cooked till the juicy droplets oozed out,
Plied me with new-brewed wine till I was tipsy.
I have promised my ox to him tomorrow.
It is a delicate matter, indeed it is."
If this is so, I say, what can I do?
With an old straw hat, with worn-out sandals,
A small figure leaves him. Only a dog barks.

I return to my snail shell of a hut. But how
Can you ask me to sleep without being sleepy?
At my north window I wait up for the dawn.
The mindless cuckoo makes my regret more keen.
Disappointed, all morning I look at the field.
The gay farmer's songs are gay no more.
A blind sigh knows no end. Only
The plow is there, shining,
Waiting to work the weed-grown field,
The plow waiting in an empty hut. . . .

Let us not worry about the spring plowing.
Long since I dreamt of rivers and lakes—
O necessary fault of mouth and belly—
So I look at the bamboo, green and green,
In the winding waters of Ch'i.[2]
O graceful gentleman, lend me an angling rod.

113

Among the flowery reeds, befriending the moon
And clear breeze, I will grow old naturally
Among the unsold breeze and unsold moon.
Mindless gulls neither invite nor reject me.
Indifferent gulls, peaceful gulls.

What noble resolve rests in me—
I have given up several remaining furrows.
I will cook gruel if there is rice,
Will starve and die, if there is not.
I will not envy others and others' goods.
You may loathe a poor and humble life:
You cannot with the hands push it aside.
You may envy a rich and noble life:
You cannot clap hands to invite it. . . .
"To be poor and yet not resent." [3]
Since I have lived thus, I am happy.
A modest life is enough for me.
To be well fed and well clad is not my dream.
In this world, calm and free,
Loyal and filial, reconciled and true,
This is the way; this is the way of life.
As for other matters, let them come as they will.

In the thirteenth year of King Injo (1635), Yi Kŭn-wŏn was appointed
Governor of Kyŏngsang Province. Moved by his good administration,
the people asked him to remain in office. The poem, which was writ-
ten in the poet's seventy-fourth year, celebrates this occasion and the
virtue of the governor.

SONG OF THE SOUTH
1635

For a thousand leagues along the southern border,
You who are unscathed by this bitter war,
Who first braved the enemy's rage,[1]
What tasks have you now and what work?
In the ruins overgrown with weeds

You build a grass roof.
You cannot till stony and barren fields,
You who have so much to do,
You are no less pressed into service.
Starving, you aged in cold and hunger;
But your constant hearts still burn.
Our beloved King bright as the sun,
With pitying love reaching wide and far,
With his deep goodness and lofty virtue,
He sent the Minister to survey the people,
And we the people who are spared see another autumn.
Bright as jade and deep as the ocean,
He felt it his duty to renew the people.[2]

You emulated former kings and widely spread the Good,
Intending to nurture His Majesty's children
In the seventy districts of Kyŏngsang Province,
You bestowed upon them great favor
Sweet as raindrops over a hundred grains,
Fresh as water to fish in a dry rut.
Hundreds of thousands of houses sing peace,
The bounteous wind blows from the east, and
Waves of favor are beyond compare.
You urge us to grow grain and mulberry trees
And warn us not to neglect spears and swords.
Man plows, woman weaves, everyone works,
Strengthens our border with bows and arrows.
With ice-cold spirit, with moon-clear breast,
You toil, loyal to the land.
Bright precepts and deep learning, you say,
Are the roots of clear politics
That serve the way of Master K'ung.
You think this is your sole mission;
So is our Way that we happily tread.
Minister, your hard work stirs us deep;

Lesser ones, too, follow your footsteps,
Love and benefit children of the south.

Once we bled, today we live in Arcadia.
Who chants in the halls covered with pine and bamboo,
Who sings by the willowed arbor,
Who plucks strings to hymn Yao and Shun
But the children of the sage King?
O wretched suitors, where do you hide?
People are wise now, so prisons are empty. . . .
Offices are in peace, so are villages.
Men walk on one side, women another,
And in the west land, rich and wide,
Farmers give the bank to each other.
Answer, cuckoo, what is this land?
Have we entered the kingdom of Chou? [3]
Folks in the south, listen to me,
Let's buy white silk and bright colors,
Paint his portrait and full figure,
Hang it on the walls of every house,
And when his face flashes through our mind,
We will see him then, our beloved Minister.

Hŏ Nansŏrhŏn
[1563–1589]

The kasa found its greatest poetess in Hŏ Nansŏrhŏn, daughter of
Minister Hŏ Yŏp, and sister of Hŏ Kyun (1569–1618), author of the
first novel written in Korean. She died young, but left a number of
beautiful verses written both in Korean and in Chinese. She is espe-
cially remembered for her two kasa poems, one of which is given here.

A WOMAN'S SORROW

Yesterday I fancied I was young;
But already, alas, I am aging.
What use is there in recalling
The joyful days of my youth?
Now I am old, recollections are vain.

Sorrow chokes me; words fail me.
When Father begot me, Mother reared me,
When they took pains to bring me up,
They dreamed, not of a duchess or marchioness,
But at least of a bride fit for a gentleman.
The turning of destiny of the three lives [1]
And the tie chanced by a matchmaker
Brought me a romantic knight,
And careful as in a dream I trod on ice.
O was it a dream, those innocent days?
When I reached fifteen, counted sixteen,
The inborn beauty in me blossomed, and
With this face and this body
I vowed a union of a hundred years.

The flow of time and tide was sudden;
The Gods too were jealous of my beauty.
Spring breezes and autumn moon,
Alas, they flew like a shuttle.
And my face that once was beautiful,
Where did it go? Who disgraced it so?
Turn away from the mirror, look no more.
Who, who will look at me now?
Blush not, my self, and reproach no one.
Don't say, "A tavern somewhere has found a friend."
When flowers smiled in the setting sun,
He rode away on a white horse
With no aim, no destination.
Where would he stop? Where should he lodge?
How far he went I know not;
I will hear nothing from him, not a word.
Yet I dare to hope he will remember me,
Though changed from what he has been.
Hush, anxious heart, hush, that longs
For the face of him who abandoned you—
Long is a day; cruel is a month.
The plum trees by the jade window
Have blossomed and scattered, spring after spring.

The winter night is bitter cold,
And snow falls thick and fast.
Long, long is a summer's day; the
Dreary rain makes my heartache keener.
And blessed spring with flowers and willows,
It, too, wears a melancholy look.
When the autumn moon enters my room
And crickets chirp on the couch,
A long sigh and salty tears
Endlessly make me recall details of the past.
It is hard to bring this cruel life to an end—
No, I must unravel my sorrow calmly.
Lighting the blue lantern, I play
A Song of Blue Lotus on the green lute,
And play it as my sorrow commands me,
As though the rain on the Hsiao and Hsiang [2]
Beat confusedly over the bamboo leaves,
As though the crane returned whooping
After a span of a thousand years.[3]
Fingers may pluck the familiar tune,
But who will listen? The room
Is empty except for the lotus-brocaded curtains.
Sing the pain that pierces my entrails,
And let it unravel sorrow inch by inch.
Oh, to sleep, and see him in a dream;
But for what reason and by what enmity
Do the fallen leaves rustling in the wind
And the insects piping among the grasses
Wake me from my wretched sleep?
The Weaver and Herdboy in the sky
Meet once on the seventh day of the seventh moon,
However hard it is to cross the Milky Way,
And never miss this yearly encounter.
But since he left me, left me alone,
What magic water separates him from me
And what makes him silent across the water?
Leaning on the balustrade, I gaze at the path he took—

Dewdrops glitter on the young grass,
Evening clouds pass by; birds sing sadly
In the thickets of green bamboos.
Numberless are the sorrowful;
But none can be as wretched as I.
Think, love, you caused me this grief;
I know not whether I shall live or die.

Anonymous
[c. 1564–1608]

RETURN TO THE MOUNTAIN

Yesterday I believed their words:
Today I find them false.
With an arrowroot hat and cotton cloth,
I return therefore to my familiar fields.
Mountains and waters are ever the same;
The pine and bamboo, too, new and fresh.
Under a humble thatched cottage
I spread a mat and lie leisurely,
Drunk from the coolness of clear breezes.
Crimson lotuses that cover the lake
Greet me, row by row, from the garden.
When day breaks, look, friends,
Children come running out to gather chestnuts.
When dogs bark at a brushwood door,
Listen to the street cries, "Fish, fish."
O neighbors and kinsmen, let's go angling,
Taking some chicken and rice wine along.
Could one miss a chance to fish at twilight?
With a sedge cape, a bamboo hat worn aslant,
Shouldering a net I start out for the stream.
Dyed by the sunset glow, I follow

The path, riding a brown calf,
A path over mountains, steep and stony.
Nature brings me wealth and warms my heart.
Lo, where the stream's margin meets the sky,
They blend into a single color.
There let's take our net, fine and white,
And cast it all along the foreshore.
Silver scales dance, jade scales jump,
Let's gather them all, both large and small,
Boil small fishes, mince larger ones;
And the wine brewed in earthenware jars,
Let's pour it full in a gourd cup,
And pass the cup from friend to friend
Until the sun bathes in the magic lake
And the moon rises over eastern valleys.
Befuddled with drink, tottering, tumbling,
When I finally reach the brushwood door,
My little son helps me, my slim wife greets me.[1]
Perhaps I alone, I alone
Am guardian of these hills and streams.

Sin Hŭm
[1566–1628]

A *chinsa* of 1585, Sin later served as Minister of Personnel and Chief
State Counselor. He was a flawless and prolific writer, and left twenty
volumes of verse and prose in Chinese. An anthology records twenty
short poems of his written between 1613 and 1623, by the Soyang
River near Ch'unch'ŏn, when he had to retire from the court to escape
from the tyrannical government of Kwanghaegun.

> I would draw her face with blood
> That lies stagnant in my heart.
> And on the plain wall of my room,
> I would hang it up and gaze.

Who has made the word, "Farewell"?
Who causes me to love and wither to death?

A rain came overnight;
Pomegranates are in full bloom.
Having rolled up a crystal screen
By the square lotus pond,
Can I unravel this deep troubled self—
Ruled by whom? Who knows?

Don't laugh, foolish people, if my
Roof beams are long or short, the pillars
Crooked. This snail shell, my grass hut,
The vines that cover it, the encircling hills
And the bright moon above,
Are mine, and mine alone.

Chang Man
[1566–1629]

He was Commanding General of the Army in the time of King Injo, and subjugated the Jurchen. He also suppressed the rebellion of a general and won a victory in 1624. Only the following poem survives.

Scared by wind and storm,
A boatman bought a horse.
But he found the winding paths
More tortuous than a heavy sea.
"Henceforth, no ship, no horse,
From now on I'll follow the plow."

Kim Tŏng-nyŏng
[1567–1596]

An excellent horseman and archer, he rendered important services during the Japanese invasion. But he died a cruel death in prison owing to the slanderous tongues of his enemies who envied his success.

> A mountain in spring catches fire.
> Unopened flowers burn.
> Yet there is water there
> To put out the flames.
> Where is the stream that can kill
> The fire that burns deep within me?

Chŏng On
[1569–1641]

He was imprisoned for ten years by Tyrant Kwanghaegun, because he criticized the latter's misgovernment; but he was released by King Injo. Later he retired to Mt. Tŏgyu and devoted his life to learned and literary leisure.

> Close the book, open the window.
> Ships float on the rivers and lakes.
> The sea gulls come and go;
> What are their wishes, complaints?
> Henceforth I will abandon ambition,
> Follow the gulls among the waters.

Kim Sang-hŏn
[1570–1652]

He was Censor General and Inspector General in the time of King Injo. When the court was about to conclude a humiliating peace with the Manchu, he opposed it and tore the royal message to pieces. After peace had been signed, the Manchu government demanded the punishment of those who had opposed the treaty; Kim was therefore transported to China and spent several years in prison. The following poem was written during his campaign against the Manchu.

> Fare you well, Mount Samgak,
> Until I see you again, River Han.
> Who would leave his birthplace,
> Leave his village and familiar faces?
> And since times look dark, turbulent,
> Who knows, I may not return again.

Kim Kwang-uk
[1580–1656]

A relative of Kim Sang-yong, he served under three kings but never brought shame upon himself. He was known for his pure and solitary life and left some twenty poems.

> Welcome, bamboo sticks,
> My true friends.
> I used you for sticks when I was young,
> But having waited long behind the window,
> Walk, now, walk on,
> Have me follow behind you.

> Bundle the piles of verbose missives,
> Burn the scrolls of empty scribbles—
> At last I ride home on a swift horse,
> Whipping the autumn winds.
> A bird newly freed cannot be happier,
> I savor freedom, sup the rustic air.

Kim Yuk
[1580–1658]

In 1644 he imported European books on the calendar, astronomy, and algebra. In 1651 he became Chief State Counselor and encouraged land reform and the minting of coins. He was one of the pioneers of social reform in Korea.

> Be sure to invite me
> When your good wine is brewed.
> I shall certainly invite you
> If flowers bloom in my arbor.
> We shall discuss, then, how to live
> A hundred years without worry.

Yun Sŏn-do
[1587–1671]

Without exception, he is the greatest poet in the *sijo* form and also in the Korean language. A *chinsa* of 1612, he did not take office because of the unsavory political situation under Tyrant Kwanghaegun. In 1616, despite his father's advice, he sent in a memorial criticizing the maladministration of the corrupt minister. The script was intercepted, and as a result his father was robbed of his position as governor, and the poet was transported to Kyŏngwŏn. There he wrote his earliest poems.

This marked the beginning of his thorny and turbulent political life that consisted of exile, recall, and retreat. In 1623, upon enthronement of King Injo, he was released. In 1628 he passed another examination and was appointed Tutor to the Heir Apparent (later Hyojong, 1619–1650–1659).

1635: Fourth Minister of Rites and Fourth Inspector; but demoted soon because of courtly intrigue.

124

1637: When the Manchu invaded, he sailed off to save Kanghwa Island from the enemy. On his way back to Cheju Island he discovered the beautiful peaks and deep gorges which he named the Fairy (or Lotus) Grotto. This was soon to become his permanent retreat.

1638: Recalled to the capital but refused; his enemies made it an issue and transported him to Yŏngdŏk. Released after a year.

1639: In spring he dreamt of the Grotto of Golden Chains and went and discovered what was to become his second favorite retreat. There, in 1642, he wrote eighteen poems.

1644: Another memorial; but again the court was against him and he therefore returned to the Fairy Grotto. Later he moved to the Grotto of Golden Chains, and in 1645 wrote eight poems there.

1650: Upon enthronement of King Hyojong, he presented another memorial. Again became a target of slander and false accusation. He retired to the Fairy Grotto and there, in 1651, wrote the *Angler's Calendar*.

1652: A special summons from King Hyojong. The poet returned to the capital but soon retired to Yangju and wrote three poems there.

1652: Entered the capital again and presented a memorial containing eight articles. The whole court denounced him, and he retired to the Grotto of Golden Chains.

1653: In the second moon he returned to the Fairy Grotto. After 1653 he moved to and fro between the two grottoes.

1657: Again at court; again released from his post but remained in the capital (1658).

1660: Issue over the length of mourning for Queen Mother of King Hyojong. The poet sent in a memorial supporting a three-year mourning for the Queen Mother; but his opponents, who insisted on a one-year mourning, won, and the poet was banished to Samsu.

1667: Released from his exile. He then returned to the Fairy Grotto and remained there until his death in 1671.

The following series of poems, entitled "Dispelling Gloom," was written in Kyŏngwŏn during his first banishment. They are the earliest poems of his that we know; nevertheless, they sing with an intensity of their own, and the native reader can anticipate in them the greatest Korean poetic genius. The young poet expresses his pure longing for the king and for his parents, and declares that his sins were nothing but expressions of his loyalty and love. In the poem, "After the Rain," the poet echoes a famous Chinese poem, traditionally attributed to Ch'ü Yüan, a loyal minister of the state of Ch'u who suffered the same predicament, in which a fisherman satirizes Ch'ü Yüan with the words: "When the Ts'ang-lang's waters are clear, I can wash my hat strings in them; when the Ts'ang-lang's waters are muddy, I can wash my feet in them." The meaning is that one should seek office at court when times are favorable and should retire when the times are troubled.

DISPELLING GLOOM
1618

Whether sad or jóyful,
Whether right or wrong,
I'll order and polish
Only my duty and the Way.
As for other matters,
I'll not split hairs.

I know it: sometimes I've been
Absurd, sometimes I've
Missed the mark. A
Foolish mind, you say.
Yet I desired always
Only to honor thee, great King.
Beware
The slanderous tongues of
Fools with more cunning.

O stream that runs in tears
Outside the cold Chinho Pavilion.
For what reasons, moving water,
Do you flow night and day?
You follow my crimson heart
And thus run on and on.

Mountain after mountain, an endless chain,
And the far-off winding of rivers.
My parents grow old far away,
In the place of my long-ago childhood.
My heart is heavy. Adrift in the sky
A wild goose floats and cackles, cackles and floats.

AFTER THE RAIN

Has a tedious rain cleared up?
Have the livid clouds rolled away?
The deep swamps in the stream in front
You say now are still as glass.
Come then, if the water is truly clear,
Let me wash my hat strings.

The following poems, "New Songs in the Mountain," were written at
the Grotto of Golden Chains. Here the poet is already a master of his
material. He was able to achieve harmony with the infinite life and
breadth of nature, and his poems are revelations of this joy he experi-
enced in his daily life.

Among mountains and streams I build
A humble thatched hut.
The ignorant mock my grass roof:
Can they fathom my true intention?
Indeed this is the fittest life
To a simple rustic mind.

———————————

Cooked barley and fresh herbs,
I have had a fair amount of them.
And by the rock in the blue stream
I play to my heart's content.
What else do I need by the water?
I long for nothing; no, nothing else.

———————————

Alone, cup in hand,
I view the distant peaks.

127

Even if my love came to me,
Would I be any happier?
The peaks neither speak nor smile;
But what happiness, O what joy!

———————

Heaven, too, detected my secret
That I am by nature slow.
Hence among all things of life
It left me not a thing.
Heaven says I shall be the guardian
To keep only the hills and waters.

MORNING MIST

High was East Mountain,
But how jealous is a morning mist.
It looms dark and devours
The majestic first peaks.
Yet the mist will soon vanish when
The sun kills it with bright rays.

SUMMER RAIN

Not to the field when it rains;
Close the door, feed the cattle.
A tiresome rain comes only once;
So now polish your plows and hoes.
Rest and wait until the rains are over,
Then we'll plow the long furrow.

SUNSET

Mountains are the more beautiful
After the sun has gone down
And it is
Twilight.
Day closes, darkness

Settles. Boy,
Watch out for tigers, now.
Let's not
Wander about in the field.

DEEP NIGHT

Close the brushwood door; winds are neighing.
Blow out the candles; night is deepening.
Let's prop on the pillows,
Let's sleep out the night.
Don't wake me until the sky
Is full of the dawn.

LAMENT FOR A FAMINE YEAR

You mock me I have done wrong
By borrowing grains from the Office.[1]
Po I and Shu Ch'i [2] gathered ferns;
I know all about their rectitude.
But do not blame me, friends;
This is a year of bad harvest.

SONGS OF FIVE FRIENDS

How many friends have I? Count them:
Water and stone, pine and bamboo—
The rising moon on the east mountain,
Welcome, it too is my friend.
What need is there, I say,
To have more friends than five?

They say clouds are fine; I mean the color.
But, alas, they often darken.
They say winds are clear; I mean the sound.
But, alas, they often cease to blow.
It is only the *water*, then,
That is perpetual and good.

Why do flowers fade so soon
Once they are in their glory?
Why do grasses yellow so soon
Once they have grown tall?
Perhaps it is the *stone*, then,
That is constant and good.

Flowers bloom when it is warm;
Leaves fall when days are cool.
But, O *pine*, how is it
That you scorn frost, ignore snow?
I know now your towering self,
Straight even among the Nine Springs.

You are not a tree, no,
Nor a plant, not even that.
Who let you shoot so straight; what
Makes you empty within?
You are green in all seasons,
Welcome, *bamboo*, my friend.

Small but floating high,
You shed light on all creation.
And what can match your brightness
In the coal dark of the night?
You look at me but with no words;
That's why, O *moon*, you are my friend.

AUTUMN NIGHT

Now that the flies are all gone,
You don't need a fly trap any more.
Now that fallen leaves sough in the wind,
Wrinkles will devour my Lord.
The moon is my friend in solitude—
It shines among the bamboo groves.

SPRING DAWN

A hard winter is over—
Where are the bitter winds now?
Spring trails over distant hills,
The mild air is still.
I will open a door and admire
The morning dyed by the spring haze.

TO AN OLD LUTE

I take out an abandoned lute,
Change the strings and play
An elegant tune of the past.
Yes, it makes a happy sound.
But who else knows the tune I played—
I have to put it back in the case.

TO MY FRIEND
1645

Heart wants to sing, but cannot sing alone;
Heart wants to dance, but dancing must have music.
 Then lute shall play,
For none but lute can strike the secret tone
 My heart would sing
 So heart and song are one;
 Then lute shall play,
For none but lute knows what is heart's desire
 So heart may spring
 Into the dance
 And beat its rhythm out.
Welcome, sweet lute, my dear, my dearest friend,
There is no hurt thy music cannot mend.

The following poems were written (1645) with a clear didactic intent
in mind. They are admonitions to the king, and it is uncertain whether
they are impromptu poems composed at an actual feast or simple ad-

131

monitions. But if we consider the fact that the poet was once Tutor of King Hyojong and distinguished himself through his innumerable memorials to the throne, it is not surprising that these poems should come from his pen.

In the first poem, "a house" alludes to the ideal state, and "the straight wood" (third line) to the benevolent government. "The work of an artisan" in the second line implies that the king should follow the way of the ancient sage kings. In the second stanza, "wine" and "broth" allude to the virtues of the king, and "yeast" and "herbs" to the wise ministers who assist in state affairs. The second poem of the second group sings moderation in pleasure. Perhaps the poet had in mind the 114th poem in the *Book of Songs*, in the first stanza of which the monitor says: "Do not be so riotous/ As to forget your home./ Amuse yourselves, but no wildness!/ Good men are always on their guard."

AT THE BEGINNING OF THE FEAST

Do you know how a house is built?
It is of course the work of an artisan.
Do you know why wood is straight?
It is planed so by the plumb line.
If you know this truth in your house,
You will then enjoy an unbroken life.

Do you know why the wine is good?
It is of course the magic of yeast.
Do you know why broth is delicious?
It is of course the magic of herbs.
If you know this truth of food,
You will then enjoy an unbroken life.

AT THE END OF THE FEAST

You may enjoy and be happy;
But should you forget your anxiety?
You may play and be merry;
But could you do so to excess?

If you know this difficulty and anxiety,
You will then enjoy an unbroken life.

You may drink wine; but
Without restraint disorder ensues.
You may dance to music; but
Without order confusion arises.
If you polish and garner your power,
You will then enjoy an unbroken life.

THE ANGLER'S CALENDAR
1651

In both Far Eastern and European literature the image of the fisher-
man occurs from time to time, but nowhere does the fisherman play
such an important role as in Korean poetry, particularly in the works
of Yun Sŏn-do. There the fisherman is a consecrated image which sym-
bolizes a pure and wise man who lives detached from the troubled
times and confused world and devotes himself only to the cultivation
of self. Yun took his inspiration partly from the previously existing
angler's songs, but what he made from them is so original that we
must give full credit to his infinitely superior technique and his control
of materials. The forty poems which cover the four seasons of the year
are products of his leisurely life at his favorite retreat, the Fairy Grotto;
but they are, at the same time, a criticism of life and of his time.

Structurally the poems differ from the common *sijo* form, and the gen-
eral pattern is as follows:

First line:	3	4	3	4
Envoi:	4	4		
Second line:	3	4	3	4
Envoi:	3	3	3	
Third line:	3	4	3	4

Therefore a pair of four syllables is added after the first line, and three
three-syllable onomatopoetic words after the second line, thus making
the total number of syllables fifty-nine. The fortieth poem in this
series has an unusual form in which the total number of syllables is
seventy-two.

According to the commentators, the poet would rise at cockcrow, drink clear wine from a jade cup, and teach his pupils. After breakfast he would drive to the arbors and pavilions in his carriage. At times he would stroll along the water, following the small wagons loaded with servants and wine that accompanied him. When he reached the Sŏnyŏm Arbor, he would have his students wait upon him. Dancing girls, riding on a small boat, would sing his angler's songs. They would also play wind and string instruments, and two parties of dancers would dance in the eastern and western terraces simultaneously. Afterward the poet would sit on a rock and fish or pick lotus flowers in the islet. Thus he would spend the day, returning to his arbor only after sunset.

The commentators hasten to add that the poet was not a great drinker, or luxurious and extravagant, but a warmhearted man versed in the human heart. When the lower class was driven into dire poverty by heavy taxation and forced labor, he would never hesitate to send in a memorial to the throne in behalf of the oppressed. He treated servants with generosity and shared his fortune with needy relatives.

Spring

The fog lifts in the stream before me
And the sun lances the back hills.
The night tide neaps, and now
The high water rushes upon the shore.
Flowers in river hamlets are fair to see,
But distant views swell my heart.

Day is warm,
Fishes float in the blue.
Weigh anchor, friends, heave it up,
Gulls appear, wing upon wing.
Heave away, ho, I have a rod;
Have you loaded a flagon of wine?

A puff of east wind ruffles
The surface of the stream into ripples.
Hoist sail, friends, spread the sail,
Let's go to West Lake by the East.
Heave away, ho, scull the boat,
Hills pass by, and more hills greet us.

Is it a cuckoo that cries?
Is it the willow that is blue?
Several roofs in a far fishing village
Swim in the mist, magnificent.
Boy, fetch an old net!
Fishes are climbing against the stream.

The sun's lanceheads are shining,
Water is calm, calm as oil.
Should we cast a net at all,
Should we drop a line on such a day?
The poem of Ch'ü Yüan [1] stirs my fancy;
I have forgotten all about fishing.

Let's return to the shore,
Twilight trails in the west.
Lower sail and scan the riverbank,
Willows and flowers are supple and sweet.
Who would envy three dukes?
Who would now think of caps and gowns?

Let us tread on fragrant grasses
And pick orchids and irises.
Stopping the boat small as a leaf,
I ask what I have taken aboard.
Nothing except smoke when I set sail,
When I row back, the moon is my tenant.

Drunk I lie asleep,
What if the boat floats downstream?
Moor the boat, Arcadia is near,
Crimson petals leap on the stream.
I am far away from red dust—
The world of men.

Let's stop angling and salute
The moon framed in raspberry canes.
Drop anchor, friends, night settles,
The cuckoo, too, sings a sweet song.

The heart shouts its peak of joy,
I have lost my way in the dark.

Tomorrow, tomorrow, we have tomorrow,
A spring night will soon see the day.
Boat ashore and rod for a cane,
Let's find our brushwood door.
This is an angler's life—
O how many sweet days, sheer content!

Summer

Tedious rain over at last,
The stream is limpid and glassy.
Entering the boat, rod at my shoulder,
I cannot still my loud heart.
Who has painted these scenes,
Smoky rivers and suspended cliffs?

Wrap the steamed rice in lotus leaves,
You need no other viands, no dainties.
I have already my blue arum hat,
Bring me, boy, a raincoat of green rushes.
Mindless gulls come and go;
Do they follow me, or I them?

A wind rises among the duckweed fronds,
Cool, cool is the raspberry window.
Let the boat float with the current,
The summer breeze is capricious.
Northern islets and southern river,
Does it matter where I go?

When the river is muddy and miry,
Don't trouble to wash your feet there.
I wish to go to the Wu River; sad
Are the angry waves of a thousand years.
Paddle the boat, then, to the Ch'u River;
But do not catch the fish of a loyal soul.[2]

136

How rare is a moss rock where
The willow groves are thick and green.
Paddle the boat, friends, and think—
Anglers don't fight for the best pool.
When you meet a hoary hermit,
Yield him the choicest stream.[3]

Moved by these precious pleasures,
I had not known day was ending.
Lower sail on the roving waves,
Let's beat the stroke with a song.
Who would know this immortal delight,
The joy of a rower in sweet songs?

The western sky burns with splendor.
Twilight will soon overtake us, lo!
Put the boat ashore and look—
Under the pine a path winds on the rock.
Do you hear the oriole's calling
Here and there in the green verdure?

Let's spread the net out on the shore
And lie under the thatched awning.
Moor the boat, friends, and rest—
Fan off mosquitoes, no, flies are worse.
Only one worry, even here,
Traitors might eavesdrop on our talk.

What will the mood of the sky be?
Night may bring wind and storm.
Drop anchor, friends, and answer,
Can one cross fields with a boat?
Fine and fresh are the magic herbs
That grow thick along the furious flumes.

Lo, my snail-shell hut
Beset from four corners by the clouds.
Put the boat ashore and climb
The stone path with bulrush fan in hand.
O the idle life of an old angler,
This is my work, this is my song.

Autumn

What is more transcendental
Than the life of a complete angler?
Mock not a hoary fisherman, friends,
He is painted by every great hand.
You say the joys of all seasons are equal?
No, autumn has most delights.

Autumn comes to a sea village,
The fishes are many and sleek.
Weigh anchor and be merry,
Merry and gay on the swelling waves.
Behind me the dusty world, but
Joy doubles as farther I sail away.

Where the white clouds take wing,
Branches sway in the breeze.
Let's go to West Lake at high tide,
And at low water to East Lake.
White duckweeds and crimson smartweeds,
They adorn every inlet.

Beyond where the wild geese fly
Unknown peaks blossom.
I will angle there, of course, but
Merry it is to be in wine.
Western skies burn in the setting sun,
A thousand hills stitch a magic scroll.

Silver scales and jade scales,
Did I have a good catch today?
Let's build a fire of reed bushes,
Charcoal the fat fishes one by one.
Pour wine from an earthenware jar,
Fill the gourd cup full to the brim.

Gently, the side wind blowing,
The boat under easy sail.
Darkness is overcoming the day,

But clear delight is there still.
Who can tire of
The fiery trees and pearly waters?

A scatter of silver dew rolls on the grass;
Moon rises.
Far and foggy is the Phoenix Pavilion,[4]
To whom should I give this light?
The white hare pounds the magic pills: [5]
Would I could feed them to the heroes.

Where is it, friends, where am I?
Is there any separation of heaven and earth?
Since the west winds cannot gall us,
No use to fan off the empty air.
Further, since I have heard no words,
Why should I bother to wash my ears? [6]

Frost falls on my cotton clothes:
I am not cold.
Don't complain that the boat is too narrow;
Compare it instead to the muddy world.
Drop anchor, we will live,
We will live this way today and ever.

I want to admire the dawn moon
In the stone cave in the bamboo grove.
But the path in the empty hills
Is hidden by fallen leaves.
Since the white clouds too follow me,
O heavy is the sedge hat on my head!

Winter

The clouds have rolled away,
The sun's rays are warm.
Heaven and earth have lost vitality;
But water as always is clear and cold.
Launch the boat, friends, and behold,
The boundless water is a silk brocade.

139

Mend your fishing line and rod,
Repair the boat with bamboo sheets.
They say the nets on the Hsiao and Hsiang,
And the Tungt'ing Lake freeze.[7]
Heave up the anchor and be happy,
No place is better than our waters.

Fishes in the shallows
Are gone to the distant swamps.
Sun shines, but shines for a moment;
So spread the sail, go out to sea—
If the bait is good,
The fat fishes will bite then, they say.

A snow settles over the night—
What new scenes before my eyes!
In front lies the water, broad and bright,
Behind are myriad hills, the jade screens.
Is it a fairy land, or Buddha's realm?
Surely it does not belong in the human world.

I have forgotten the net and rod,
Uselessly beat the edge of the boat.
How many times have I wished,
Wished to follow the stream ahead?
What if a gale should rise
And set my boat in motion.

The crows hastening to their nests,
How many have flown overhead?
Darkness envelops our homeward path,
The evening snow lies thick.
Who will attack the Oya Lake
And avenge the shame of soldier trees? [8]

Red cliffs and green canyons
Enfold us like a painted screen.
Stop the boat, what does it matter
If I catch any fish or not?
In an empty boat, wearing my reed hat,
I sit alone and my heart beats fast.

By the river a lone pine,
How mighty, how towering.
Do not scorn the rough clouds,
They screen the mad world from us.
Do not deplore the storm and waves—
They arrest the bustle of the world.

People used to praise my way of life
In the pious land of the fairies.[9]
Drop anchor and tell me, who wore
The sheepskin cloth at Ch'ili Shore?
And during three thousand six hundred days
Let us count our trade blessed.[10]

Day closes, time to feast and rest.
Put the boat ashore and come, elated—
Let's tread the path where the snow
Is strewn with crimson petals.
Lean from the pine window and gaze
As the moon crosses the western sky.

The poet was summoned by King Hyojong in 1652 and entered the
capital after seventeen years of absence. But his political enemies de-
famed and rejected him, and the poet retired to his country retreat,
after a month's stay at court, and wrote the following poems. Here "the
Jade Emperor" is King Hyojong himself, and "a host of spirits" are his
opponents. In the last stanza he laments the absence of wise ministers
who could repair "the Pavilion of White Jade," namely, who could
save the state from the evils of the times. The poet planned to advise
the King of capable men and capital plans, but filibusters did not allow
him any opportunity.

THE DISAPPOINTING JOURNEY
1652

Am I awake? Am I asleep?
I ascend to the city of white jade.
The Jade Emperor himself welcomes me;
But a host of spirits envy my presence.

141

Forgo them all, my only joys are
The five lakes and smoky moon.[1]

I dream a dream in a broken sleep,
Enter the Palace of Twelve Pavilions.[2]
The Jade Emperor smiles at me; but
A host of spirits scold my intent.
When can I ask then
About the billions of souls on earth?

When heaven is torn to rags
What art can stitch it together?
When the Jade Pavilion falls
What art can raise it up?
I cannot appeal to the Jade Emperor;
I return without opening my lips.

Yi Myŏng-han
[1595–1645]

Senior Academician and Minister of Personnel, who distinguished himself during the Manchu invasion. He was poor but never failed to have wine for his friends. His contemporaries praise his poems for their audacity and subtlety of expression and sweetness of melody.

Do not draw back your sleeves and go,
My own,
With tears I beg you.
Over the long dike green with grass
Look, the sun goes down.
You will regret it, lighting the lamp
By the tavern window,
Sleepless, alone.

If my dreams
Left their footprints on the road
The path beneath my love's window

Would be worn down, though it is stone.
Alas, in the country of dream
No roads endure, no traces remain.

Song Si-yŏl
[1607–1689]

A pernicious enemy of Yun Sŏn-do, he was active in party strife, and many lost their lives because of his machinations. At last, he was sentenced to death, and he took poison and died.

Mountains are natural, natural,
Waters, too, natural, natural.
Between the natural mountains, waters,
I myself am natural, natural.
This body that grew naturally,
Will no doubt naturally age.

Kang Paeng-nyŏn
[1603–1681]

Born in Chinju, his political career covered a long span of some fifty years. He was a flawless minister who taught loyalty and filial piety, and loved the people. After his death, his name was recorded in the section of unsullied officials in the histories, and King Sukchong (1661–1675–1720) honored him with the posthumous title of Chief State Counselor.

My fair face in youthful years,
O it grew old because of love.
Would she know me, would she,
If she saw me now?
If my love knew my old-man's face
I'd die without a care.

143

Prince Pongnim
[1619–1659]

Second son of King Injo, he ascended the throne as King Hyojong. He spent his youth as a hostage in China and wanted to wipe out the shame of Manchu subjugation. He planned a march into the north with several ministers but did not see his wish executed.

What amuses you in the sound
Of blue rain on the clear stream,
O flowers and trees of the hill?
You shake and laugh, laugh and shake.
Take pleasure, then, while you may;
Only a few more days of the spring breezes.

Nam Ku-man
[1629–1711]

He was Chief State Counselor and served under Kings Hyojong and Sukchong. He is famous for this poem alone.

The eastern window pales.
The lark sings; day breaks.
Cowherd, little servant,
Have you not yet risen, not yet?
When will you sow the broad field,
Deep furrowed, running over the hill?

Ku Yong
[seventeenth century]

Even the wide ocean has dried up
And the sand has formed an island,
And the senseless grass grows thick,
Renewed and renewing year after year;
Why, why does he not return,
Our prince who has left us?

Yu Hyŏng-nyŏn
[1616–1680]

He distinguished himself as Military Commander, but owing to a political change at court, fell into disgrace and was sentenced to death.

A swift horse grows stiff, unridden,
A sharp sword gathers rust, unused.
"Time and tide wait for no man."
My hair will soon be white.
When, when am I going to return
The favor of my lord?

Yi T'aek
[1651–1719]

He passed the military examination in 1676 and served as Navy Commander.

O roc, don't ridicule the small black birds:
You and the little birds both fly way up in the clouds,
You're a bird,
And they're birds.
Really, I can't see much difference between you!

Chu Ŭi-sik
[1675–1720]

He was appointed as Prefect in the time of King Sukchong, but soon
retired in order to be away from party strife at court. His poems are
either Taoist or hedonistic.

> A boy stopped outside my window,
> Told me it was the New Year.
> So I look out my eastern window—
> The sun rises as of old, unchanged.
> Look, boy, it's the same old sun;
> Don't bother me now, come some other time.

Kim Sam-hyŏn
[c. 1675–1700]

Son-in-law of Chu Ŭi-sik, whom he followed in writing poems in praise
of rustic solitude.

> Having dozed in the pinewood
> I awake, sleepy from drink.
> The setting sun is over the riverbank,
> And look, sea gulls fly in and out.
> Yes, perhaps only I
> Know the beauty of these hills and streams.

Kim Yu-gi
[c. 1675–1700]

A poet and musician, he flourished in the reign of King Sukchong and
left some dozen poems.

> Don't boast of your new dresses,
> Peach tree and plum tree in blossom.

Look at the pine and bamboo,
Green, green in sun or in snow.
Those noble, lofty presences—
They don't change with the weather.

Kim Su-jang
[b. 1690]

Together with Kim Ch'ŏn-t'aek, he is one of the representative poets
of the eighteenth century. He was also known as a good teacher of
poetry and music and a compiler of the Haedong kayo or Songs of
Korea (1763), in which he is represented by 117 poems.

In a grass hut, far from anyone,
I sit alone.
The clouds are falling asleep
To the quiet sound of my song.
O who else knows this blessedness,
Who says there is my equal?

Yi Chŏng-bo
[1693–1766]

A chinsa of 1721, he opposed party strife and remained at court for
thirty-five years in order to restore order in the government. The Songs
of Korea records seventy-eight poems of his, all produced in his later
years.

The Milky Way climbs higher, and
Wild geese are cackling overhead.
Last night, coming in out of the frosty air,
The hair below my ears looked gray.
A feeble and grizzled look in the glass—
Who is that? Alas, is that I?

Yi Chae
[c. 1725–1776]

A descendant of the royal family, he has a place in Korean history not because of his birth, but because of his literary accomplishment.

> The morning star has set. A lark
> Rises out of the long grass as I take
> My hoe and close my cottage door.
> My cloth breeches already are wet with dew.
> Boy, if these were peaceful times,
> Who'd be fretting about his wet clothes?

Kim Sŏng-gi
[c. 1725–1776]

He was first a famous archer, but changed to the lute and became a first-class musician.

> Having given up this life of care,
> A bamboo stick in hand, wearing sandals,
> I go to the West Lake
> With a six-stringed lute.
> The gulls fly among the reeds—
> O my bosom friends, you greet me.

Kim Ch'ŏn-t'aek
[c. 1725–1776]

He was a famous singing policeman, a noted poet and compiler of the *Eternal Language of Green Hills* (1728), the first anthology of the *sijo*. His friends included, among others, Kim Su-jang, in whose anthology he is represented by fifty-seven poems.

> I have tried both pen and sword.
> I am not finished; what did I attain?
> Truly, I have spent fifty long springs,
> Spent these years, dull and dry.

Forgo them all, I say. Is there
Any mountain that would deceive me?

———————————

Stay, white gulls, talk awhile,
Stay aloft and speak—
In what beautiful bays, along
What sunny shores have you been wandering?
Speak of your journeys in subtle cries
Until I take wing and follow you.

———————————

Having given my clothes to a boy,
To have him pawn them at the tavern,
And looking up to heaven,
I question the moon.
Who is Li Po, that ancient drunkard,
What is he compared with me?

Anonymous

SPRING SLEEP

I sleep in spring and awake late,
And half open the bamboo window.
In the garden, flowers are bright,
Butterflies gently pause in mid-air.
Willows along the stream
Are veiled by the dim spring mist.
Festively I drink by the window
Two and three cups of unripe wine,
Elated, full of high spirits.
Unable to control this joy of mine,
Whipping a white horse with a whip of gold,
I ask the way to a green tavern.
The fragrance of flowers assaults me,
And moonlight floods the garden.
There like a mad man and drunken

I pass a night with mighty heart.
I pace up and down, look right and left,
And when standing there in blessed mood,
Still, O still—on a high pavilion
Of green tiles and crimson rails,
A beautiful woman in green and red
Opens gently a gauze window.
She lifts her jade face
And smiles at me and welcomes me—
Or is she merely displaying her airs and graces?
With a solitary song I greet her,
The tune that quickens the joy of spring.[1]
On the Terrace of Love lofty as clouds,
Sweet is the dream of love, O sweet.
Vast is Love; affinity, too, is deep.
This love and this affinity,
Is there anything to compare?[2]

Anonymous

PLEASURE IN THE MOUNTAINS

Flowers are bright in the spring fields,
All creation is green in harmonious air.
Friends, let's go to the mountain and river
With bamboo sticks, straw sandals, a gourd.
We enter deep into the hills and waters....
The pine and bamboo form a dense forest;
The hills are aflame, boast of the season.
Among strange flowers and precious plants,
Drunken butterflies wander.
Orioles glitter among the willows,
Butterflies snow among the flowers.
Joyous season it is; O pink peach blossoms.

From a boat that follows the stream
I scan the Peach Blossom Spring,
The silver thread of green tamarisk,[1]
The five willows of T'ao Ch'ien the poet.[2]
While swallows dart, spurning the waves,
A host of wild geese pass among white clouds.
Where do you go over the forlorn hills?
Layer upon layer, distant mountains unfold,
At each turn, strange stones appear.
Only the twisted pines among the untamed winds
Boldly sway in graceful measure.
Waters fall in cascade from the precipice,
As though a crystal screen had been unfolded,
A river from this valley, a freshet from that;
Ten rivers gather blindly and madly,
Jumping, clashing, gushing, ringing,
Ramping against the rock, scattering silver pieces.[3]
Listen, cuckoos tell of bygone days,
And nightingales foretell abundant harvest.
When the sunrise and sunset lie before you,
What fairer scene could your heart desire?

Anonymous
[c. 1725]

SONG OF THE LANTERN FEAST

On the day of the first full moon,
The children play, enjoying the moon,
They play, stamping on the bridge.[4]
But where is he, ah, where is my Love?
Alas, he is not on the bridge.

On the day of the Clear and Bright,
The lusty sap stirs the trees;
Young buds spring among the grass;
Everything grows in harmony—

151

But where is he, ah, where is my Love?
He knows not, alas, that spring is here.

On the third day of the third moon,
Swallows come, come from the south;
And the wild geese from the Hsiao and Hsiang,
They say they must bid us farewell.
Pear and peach trees are in bloom,
Apricot petals fall on the grass,
They are scattered, whispering and falling.
But where is he, ah, where is my Love?
He knows not this is the season of flowers.

On the eighth day of the fourth moon
I climb the terrace to see the lanterns,
Lit at sundown, far and near.
Fish lanterns and dragon lanterns,
Phoenix lanterns and crane lanterns,
A heron and the southern star;
Fairy lanterns and drum lanterns,
Watermelon and garlic lanterns,
A fairy messenger in the lotus,
A celestial nymph on a fabulous bird,
Ship lanterns and house lanterns,
Egg lanterns and bottle lanterns,
Mask-play lanterns and shadow lanterns,
Closet, sedan, and rail lanterns,
A masked hero riding a lion,
Straw puppets on wolves and tigers—
And the sun lanterns and moon lanterns
Shine on the lanterns that roll on the ground,
And beyond the arch of the Plow
Rises the moon over East Mountain,
And below, windows are lit here and there.
But where is he, ah, where is my Love?
He knows not how the lanterns shine.

On the fifth day of the fifth moon,
Other folks' children install a swing.

Gaily they play on the swings, up and down,
Hurtling downward, zooming upward—
But where is he, ah, where is my Love?
He knows not it is the season of swings.

Kim U-gyu
[fl. 1725–1776]

After the rain in the rivers and lakes,
Waters and sky are of one color.
Having loaded a boat with wine,
I wet my line, follow the water.
Who is welcoming me amid the reeds—
Is it not the sea gulls, calling?

Cho Myŏng-ni
[fl. 1697–1756]

Four poems survive.

Wild geese have passed overhead;
The first frosts have come.
Long, long is the autumn night;
The melancholy of the traveler is intense.
When the bright moon shines,
I am back in my home garden.

Pak Hyo-gwan
[c. 1850–1880]

A poet and compiler of the Kagok wŏllyu or Source Book of Songs
(1876), he flourished in the reigns of Kings Ch'ŏlchong (1831–1850–
1863) and Kojong (1853–1864–1907). He was a favorite of Hŭngsŏn

taewŏn'gun (1820–1898), Kojong's father, who conferred upon him a pen name, "Unae" ("Cloudy Cliff"). He was loved by officials at court and by his disciples, and was known as "Mr. Pak" among lovers of poetry.

> If my lovesick dream became a cricket
> In the long, long autumn night,
> It would enter my love's room
> And wake her from her sleep,
> The sound sleep that has forgotten me.

An Min-yŏng
[c. 1870–1880]

He was a disciple of Pak Hyo-gwan and helped him to compile the *Source Book of Songs*, in which he is represented by twenty-six poems. He is said to have had a better singing voice than his master. He is a poet of flowers, and a group of ten poems is addressed to the plum blossoms.

> O cold attitude, jewel form,
> Splendor of snow among the snows.
> You bring a sweet scent,
> Invite the moon at dusk.
> Your elegance, can it be matched?
> Pure and noble plum blossoms.

> The wintry wind chases the snow,
> Knocks on the mountain window.
> A draught from the door
> Overcomes the sleeping plum blossoms.
> But however much you despoil the flowers,
> Can you prevent the approach of spring?

> Speak, chrysanthemum, why do you shun
> The orient breezes of the third moon?

154

"I had rather freeze in a cruel rain
Beside the hedge of dried sticks,
Than humble myself to join the parade:
Those flowers of a fickle spring."

Anonymous *Sijo* Poems

The quality of the *sijo* cannot be studied fully without a due consideration of many anonymous poems. Unknown authors contributed as much to the perfection of this form as did known writers. In Korean poetry, as in the poetry of Greece, Persia, and China, anonymous writers have composed many poems of the most striking merit. At least one-third of the corpus of the *sijo* recorded in anthologies is by anonymous writers.

The subject matter of anonymous *sijo* covers as wide a range as those we have just seen. But the favored topic seems to be love. The poems on this theme tend to be more personal and more realistic. Tension was achieved by the power of the drama of the mind, the quality of inner conflict. In order to reveal this quality of experience, poets chose simple, direct, at times even naïve, language.

The wisdom these anonymous poems contains is often developed in naïve terms: probably the origin of these poems lay in folk songs; they reflect the traditional wisdom shared by a people rooted deeply in the community. For this reason it has a sensuous quality, more indigenous than in other poems, and in that sense more persistent and durable. The native reader of these poems smells the Korean soil and feels the Korean sky above it.

Were you to become I, and I you,
Born in each other's world,
You would have a hard time of it
And suffer a heartbreak as I have.
You would know then, taught in turn,
How I have grieved all my life.

In the wind that blew last night,
Peach blossoms fell, scattered in the garden.
A boy came out with a broom,
Intending to sweep them away.
No, do not sweep them away, no, no.
Are fallen flowers not flowers?

If flowers bloom, we demand the moon.
If the moon lights up, we ask for wine;
And when we have all these at once,
Still there is something missing.
O, when can I drink a night away,
Enjoying moon and flowers and friend?

A flickering shadow haunts the window.
I start up, open, go out.
Only clouds passing the misty moon—
No, it was not the one for whom I've been waiting.
I'm lucky, night doesn't look in to laugh;
But what if it happened in broad daylight?

A horse neighs, wants to gallop:
My love clings to me, begs me to stay.
The moving sun has crossed the hill.
I have a thousand miles to go.
My love, do not stop me:
Stop the sun from setting!

The faint moon in a heavy frost;
A solitary wild goose flies cackling.
Love, I fancied it brought me news.
Was it a letter from my love, indeed?
No, I hear only the bird
Among the clouds, incredibly far.

In the valley where the stream leaps,
Having built a grass hut by the rock,
I till the field under the moon,

Among the vast clouds I lie.
Heaven and earth advise me
To age together with them.

Let's go, butterflies, to the green meadow,
Swallowtails, you go too.
If the sun sets on the way,
Let's lodge among flowers.
If they receive us poorly,
Let's sleep on the leaves.

O dream, foolish dream, think now,
You sent him away when he came.
Better to waken than dream he leaves me.
But ah, to wake and find him gone—
Henceforth, wake me, shake me awake,
Having seized him if he came.

I have lived anxious and hurt.
Enough, enough, I would rather die,
Become the spirit of the cuckoo,
When the moon is on the bare hills,
And sing with bitter tears
Sing to him my forbidden hopes.

What was love in fact, what was it?
Was it round, was it square?
Was it long, was it short?
More than an inch, more than a yard?
It seems of no great length,
But somehow I don't know where it ends.

O love, round as the watermelon,
Do not use words sweet as the melon.
What you have said, this and that,
Was all wrong, you mocked me.
Enough, your empty talk
Is hollow, like a preserved melon.

Alas, they deceived me—
The autumn moon and the spring breeze.
Since they came around in every season
I believed they were sincere and sure.
But they left me graying hair,
And followed the boys and went away.

The incense is burnt out in the censer;
The water clock tells us night is deep.
Where have you been half the night,
In what cheerful company?
You return to sound me on my sorrow,
When the moon climbs up the railing.

I reviewed my heart one day, and
Found a piece of it missing.
I have not fasted,
But—was it taken off of itself?
Think, love, you produced this sickness;
You can cure me, you alone can.

Mind, let me ask you, how it is
You're still so young?
When I am well on in years
You, too, should grow old.
Why, if I followed your lead, Mind,
People would laugh me to scorn.

They say in this world, we have
Many remedies and brilliant swords.
But no sword to cut off this love,
No remedies that make me forget him.
I'll not forget until I am dead,
Cut off this tie, forever bury him.

TWENTIETH-CENTURY

POETRY

1900—

Ch'oe Nam-sŏn
[1890–1957]

The greatest historian of modern day, Ch'oe edited Korean classics and standard histories of Korea. One of the thirty-three patriots, he signed the "Declaration of Independence," which he wrote himself. He is the pioneer of free verse in Korea.

FROM THE SEA TO CHILDREN

The sea—a soaring mountain—
Lashes and crushes mighty cliffs of rock.
Those flimsy things, what are they to me?
"Know ye my power?" The sea lashes
Threateningly, it breaks, it crushes.

No fear assaults, no terror
Masters me. Earth's power and pride
Are tedious toys to me. All that the earth
Imagines mighty is to me no more
Than a mere feather floating by.

Who has not bowed his head
Before my sovereignty, let him come forth.
Princes of earth, challenge me if you will.
First Emperor, Napoleon, are you my adversary?
Come, come then, compete with me.

Perched on a small hill or possessed
Of an islet or a patch of land,
Thinking that you alone reign supreme
In that kingdom small as a grain,
Approach me, coward, gaze on me.

Only the arching vault of sky, my kin,
Can equal me, only the vast sky,
Whose bright image my waters beat.
Free from sin, free from stain
It ignores earth's little multitudes.

I scorn the world's madness,
The overweaning men who seek to use me.
My love (brave children)—that is given
Only to those who come to me with love.
Come, children, let me kiss you and embrace you.

Han Yong-un

A Buddhist priest, and one of the most original Korean poets of this century. Born in 1879, he shaved his head at the age of twenty-eight. Yong-un is his priestly name; his pen name is "Manhae" ("Ten Thousand Seas"). He signed the "Declaration of Independence" as one of thirty-three patriots representing the Buddhist world, and was imprisoned for three years. He died in 1944. In 1962 the government recognized his brilliant services for the cause of Korean independence and posthumously honored him. In addition to a collection of poetry, *The Silence of Love*, his works include four novels and treatises on Buddhism.

I DO NOT KNOW

Whose footstep is that paulownia leaf that falls silently in the windless air, drawing a perpendicular?

Whose face is that piece of blue sky peeping through the black clouds, chased by the west wind after a dreary rain?

Whose breath is that unnamable fragrance, born amid the green moss in the flowerless deep forest and trailing over the ancient tower?

Whose song is that winding stream gushing from an unknown source and breaking against the rocks?

Whose poem is that twilight that adorns the falling day, treading over the boundless sea with lotus feet and caressing the vast sky with jade hands?

The ember becomes oil again.

Ah, for whose night does this feeble lantern keep vigil, the unquenchable flame in my heart?

No Cha-yŏng

Born in 1898, he worked as a journalist and editor. He died of consumption in 1940. His works include *Flames of Love*, *A Maiden's Wreath*, and *The White Peacock*.

GRAPES

Bunches of dark grapes, purple pearls.
My love, your eyes look out from each cluster,
I kiss them as I pick the purple fruit.

Vines summered the pearls from a cruel season,
Secret passion scorched your crimson body.
I hold the mellow grapes in my palms.

Bunches on the platter are smoky stars,
At night I draw your face in my room,
Salting the sad grapes with my tears.

Yi Sang-hwa

He was born in Taegu in 1900. In January, 1922, he and a group of fellow poets founded a literary journal, *Paekcho* or *White Tide*. After a career in teaching, he led a wandering life in China. He died in 1943, under pressure from the Japanese police. In 1948 his friends erected a monument to his memory in Taegu. This was the first such monument raised by other writers to the memory of a modern Korean poet.

DOES SPRING COME TO STOLEN FIELDS?

The land is no longer our own.
Does spring come just the same

to the stolen fields?
On the narrow path between the rice fields
where blue sky and green fields meet and touch,
winds whisper to me, urging me forward.
A lark trills in the clouds
like a young girl singing behind the hedge.
O ripening barley fields, your long hair
is heavy after the night's rain.
Lightheaded, I walk
lightly, shrugging my shoulders, almost
dancing to music the fields are humming—
the field where violets grow, the field
where once I watched a girl planting rice, her hair
blue-black and shining—
                 I want
a scythe in my hands, I want
to stamp on this soil, soft as a plump breast,
I want to be working the earth and streaming with sweat.

What am I looking for? Soul,
my blind soul, endlessly darting
like children at play by the river,
answer me: where am I going?
Filled with the odor of grass, compounded
of green laughter and green sorrow,
I walk all day, lamely, as if possessed
by the spring devil:
for these are stolen fields, and our spring is stolen.

Pak Chong-hwa

A poet and patriot, he was born in 1901. In 1922 he was a member of the staff of the magazine *Paekcho* or *White Tide*. His poetry is of the symbolist school. He has published several volumes of verse and historical novels, including one on the Japanese invasion of 1592. He was awarded the 1954 literature prize of the Korean Academy of Arts.

KORYǑ CELADON

Bluish green with subtle lines,
O supple smooth curving,
Like a bodhisattva's shoulders,
Grace and elegance combined.
A swallow spurns the waves
And cleaves the April breeze.
But wake!—for this is Koryǒ celadon,
This was ours for a thousand years.

Depth of color, softly shaded;
Iridescent kingfisher;
Blue sky glimpsed through autumn clouds
As the rain squall passes on;
Or a white cloud, fresh with dew,
Wings its way on high.
But wake!—for this is Koryǒ celadon,
This was ours for a thousand years.

Flagons, pitchers, bowls and dishes,
Ink slabs, censers, incense boxes,
Vases, wine cups, pillows, drums;
They are clay—but they are jade!

Pressed designs of clouds and waves,
Inlaid gems and Seven Treasures,
White cranes standing among flowers,
Buddhist figures, lines of verse:
Work of craftsman and of painter,
Art of sculptor in crude clay.
But wake!—for this is Koryǒ celadon,
This was ours for a thousand years.

Sim Hun

A poet, novelist, and dramatist, he was born in 1904 in Seoul and had a career in journalism. He died in 1937 and left a volume of verse and several novels, the most celebrated of which is *Evergreen* (1935).

WHEN THAT DAY COMES

When that day comes
Mt. Samgak will rise and dance,
the waters of Han will rise up.

If that day comes before I perish,
I will soar like a crow at night
and pound the Chongno bell with my head.
The bones of my skull
will scatter, but I shall die in joy.

When that day comes at last
I'll roll and leap and shout on the boulevard
and if joy still stifles within my breast
I'll take a knife

and skin my body and make
a magical drum and march with it
in the vanguard. O procession!
Let me once hear that thundering shout,
my eyes can close then.

Kim Sowŏl
[1903–1934]

The most famous folk poet of this century. Many of his poems have
been set to music. His name was Kim Chŏng-sik; Sowŏl was his pen
name.

THE AZALEA

You're sick and tired of me.
When you go
I'll bid you goodbye without saying a word.

I'll gather
azaleas on Yak Mountain,
the burning azaleas of Yŏngbyŏn,
and strew them in your path.

Tread gently, please,
step by step, softly,
on the flowers of dedication.

You're sick and tired of me.
When you leave
I'll not weep though I die.

INCANTATION

O name broken piecemeal,
strewn in the empty void.
Nameless name, deaf and dumb,
that suffers me to die as I call it.

The last word carved in my heart
was never spoken in the end.
O you that I love,
O you that I love.

Crimson sun hangs on the west peak,
the deer bell and call sadly.
There on the sheer steep peak
I call, call your empty name.

Until sorrow chokes me and unmans me,
still I will call your name.
My voice goes aslant rejected,
lost between heaven and earth.

Were I to become a stone,
I would die calling your name.
O you that I love,
O you that I love.

Yi Yuksa

He was born in 1905 and graduated from Peking University in sociol-
ogy. Toward the end of the Second World War, he entered Peking

again, was seized by the Japanese police for his patriotic activities, and died in prison in 1944. His name was Yi Hwal; Yuksa was his pen name.

THE LAKE

Although my mind would like to turn and run,
My eyes still meditate, stubborn as winds.

At times I invite swans, then set them free,
Embracing the shores I lie and weep at night.

As I ruminate on the shadow of a dim star,
The purple mist settles down like a thinking cap.

THE SUMMIT

Beaten by the bitter season's whip,
At last I am driven to this north.

I stand upon the sword-blade frost,
Where numb sky and plateau merge.

I do not know where to bend my knees,
Nor where to lay my vexed steps.

I cannot but close my eyes and think—
Winter, O winter is a steel rainbow.

DEEP-PURPLE GRAPES

In July in my native land,
The blue grapes ripen in the sun.

Village wisdom clusters around the vines,
The distant skies enter into each berry.

The sea below the sky opens its bosom,
A white sail moves toward the shore.

The traveler I long for would come then,
Wrapping his wayworn body with a blue robe.

If only I could share those grapes with him,
I don't care if the dew wets my hands.

168

Child, take out a white gauze handkerchief,
Spread it on the silver platter on our table.

Yu Ch'i-hwan

Born in 1908, he graduated from Yŏnhŭi College (now Yŏnse University). He won the 1949 literary award of the city of Seoul and the 1961 literature prize of the Korean Academy of Arts. He died in 1967.

FLOWERS

Autumn has come, and from somewhere the children
bring home flower seeds.
They count them over, arrange them
one by one:
balsam, cockscomb, smartweed,
morning glory.
         After homework,
when they are ready for sleep,
even in bed they talk about seeds:
If only we had a garden to plant them.
Meanwhile, night deepens; and when their mother
covers them up with straw mats,
these poor tired flowers fall asleep, each embracing
a fabulous flower bed.

Kim Ki-rim

Champion of modernism in Korean poetry, Kim has been active in the introduction of twentieth-century Anglo-American poetry. His early poetry is imagist. Later he began also to publish criticism influenced by the work of the "New Critics."

A TALE

On the beach embroidered
With white dunes and clouds,
The boy and aronia bloom
In the burning noon.

In many cobalt layers,
Ozone is bluer than the sky,
And under the toes like maple roots
The sea resounds like an organ.

No boundary exists between
The noon and dream.
Here the pure properties are
Pebbles, shells, and white chart.

Dewy pupils are the pearls
Gathered overnight in the coral bush,
And the ears echo, like a shell,
The metallic winds.

The shoulders ache;
The white wings grow.
Throbbing veins must be
Connected to the wave.

Paek Sŏk

Born in 1912, he studied in Tokyo and later taught at a high school.
His name is Paek Ki-haeng; Paek Sŏk or Paeksŏk ("White Stone") is
his pen name.

DOG

In the village where tallow candles twinkle in the dish and castor
oil burns in the bull's horn, barking of dogs on a winter night
brings welcome news.

Someone must be out on this terrible night, sliding along the up-
per and lower village—dogs bark.

If someone crosses the hills to bring home vermicelli to cook with
a pheasant netted by day, then dogs bark.

A night when pickled turnips and cabbages burst the cap of the round jar—

When grandfather went out at night to bring vermicelli home, I, putting on my grandmother's glasses, heard the dogs bark, bark.

Kim Kwang-gyun

Born in 1913, he worked as a company employee, before he established a manufacturing business. Most of his earlier and best poetry is collected in Gaslight (1939) and Ports of Call (1947).

DESSIN

Against the thin incense and twilight,
Telegraph poles lean one by one,
And night alights on the overhead rail.

Clouds
Are a bouquet of roses
Painted at random on purple paper.

Meadow flags and apple boughs
Tremble at the gentle breeze
On a lonely trail.

THE SUNFLOWER

Here is the white sunflower—
Its tyranny caused a small village to fade;
In the old house by the village road,
A hoary mother turned a water wheel.

When twilight tumbled down the purple lane,
The rushes by the stream
Shook their heads and wept.

To light the lamp on our father's tomb,
Nightly I led my blind sister by the hand
And crossed the track dyed by the moonlight.

171

Chang Man-yŏng

Born in 1914, he studied in Tokyo. He is a champion of imagist poetry and has published three volumes of verse and edited an anthology of modern Korean poetry.

MOON, GRAPES, LEAVES

Suni, in the insect-tormented classic garden,
the moonlight rushes in like an angry lake.

The moon sits mute in my garden,
more fragrant than any fruit.

Like the waves of the Eastern Sea
blue
autumn
night.

Sweet grapes are dyed by the moon's ray,
the moon-fed grapes burst in the night.

Suni, look, young leaves behind the vines,
bedewed by the moon, lonesome leaves.

Sŏ Chŏng-ju

Born in 1915 in the South, he studied Buddhism when he was young. He has published several volumes of verse and edited two anthologies of modern poetry.

HIGH NOON

Along a path among the crimson flower beds,
Where flowers of oblivion conspire death,

My love runs away, calls me
Along the path that coils like a drunk snake.

The scented blood dripping from my nose
Into my palms, I follow her

In the boiling noon, still as night
Burning, burning, two of us—

SELF-PORTRAIT

Father was a serf, seldom came home at night.
At home my grandmother, old as
The shriveled root of leek,
And a blossoming date tree.
Big with child, Mother wanted just one apricot.

I was a mother's son with dirty fingernails
Under a lamp by the mud wall.
With bushy hair and staring eyes,
I am said to resemble Grandpa on Mother's side,
Who in 1894 went to sea and never returned.

For twenty-three years the wind has reared two-thirds of me,
And the world has become a more embarrassing place.
Some have read a convict in my eyes,
Others an idiot in my mouth.
Yet I will repent nothing.

At each dawn, brightly assailing,
The dews of poetry settled on my brow,
Mixed with drops of blood.
And I have come this far panting
Like a sick dog with his tongue hanging out
In the sun and in the shade.

TO A FRIEND

Having had my hair newly cropped,
I look different from other poets.
How good is the sky after
I have laughed with my adamantine teeth.
My fingernails, too, thicken like tortoise shells.

Friend, no more talk about the girls
Sweet as nightingales,
Until we meet again in the other world.
Like Li Po with a slender neck,
Why do we have to be so aristocratic?

I spend the moonlit night of Verlaine
Twining ropes with a servant boy.
Should I yet hear the nightingale's songs,
Why then, I'll cut off my shameful ears.

Pak Mogwŏl

He was born in 1916 and was a schoolmaster for awhile. He has published several volumes of verse and collections of children's songs for which he is well known. His name is Pak Yŏng-jong; Mogwŏl is his pen name.

TRAVELER

Beyond the ferry,
on a path through the wheat fields

Moves a swift traveler
like a moon in the clouds.

Along the one-way path,
three hundred leagues to the south,

Sky burns over a village
where new wine sings aloud.

A traveler plods on,
like a moon in the clouds.

APRIL

On a lonely peak,
feathery crests of pine needles.

174

When a cuckoo laments
a long day in the leap month,

in a woodman's hut,
behind the half door,

a blind girl gives ear,
pressed to the gate pillar.

Pak Tu-jin

One of the "Southern Trio" (the others being Pak Mogwŏl and Cho
Chi-hun), he was born in 1916 and worked in a managerial position
until 1945. He has published several volumes of poetry.

PEACHES ARE IN BLOOM

Tell them that the peaches are in bloom and the apricots.
By the warm home you left abandoned, and now on that hedge
   once recklessly trampled, cherries and plums ripen.
Bees and butterflies praise the day, and the cuckoo sings by moon-
   light.
In the five continents and six oceans, O Ch'ŏl, beyond the hoofed
   clouds and winged skies, into which corner shall I look in
   order to stand face to face with you?
You are deaf to the sad note of my flute in the moonlit garden, and
   to my songs of dawn on the green peak.
Come, come quickly, on the day when the stars come and go, your
   scattered brothers return one by one. Suni and your sisters,
   our friends, Maksoe and Poksuri, too, return.
Come, then, come with tears and blood, come with a blue flag,
   with pigeons and bouquets.
Come with the blue flag to the valley full of peach and apricot
   blossoms.
The south winds caress the barley fields where you and I once
   frolicked together, and among the milky clouds larks sing
   loud.

175

On the hill starred with shepherd's purse, lying on that green hill,
   Ch'öl, you will play on the grass flute, and I will dance a
   fabulous roc dance.
And rolling on the grass with Maksoe, Tori, and Poksuri, let us,
   let us unroll our happy days, rolling on the blue-green young
   grass.

Yun Tong-ju

Born in Kando in 1917, he attended Yönhŭi College in Seoul, and
later Doshisha University in Kyoto, Japan. In July, 1943, while he was
still a student in Kyoto, he was seized by the Japanese police on a
charge of patriotic activities for the independence of Korea. He died
in the Fukuoka prison in Kyushu in January, 1945. A collection of his
works was published posthumously under the title of Sky, Wind, Stars
and Poetry.

SELF-PORTRAIT

I go round the foot of a mountain to seek for a lonesome well by
   the field and look into it without words.

In the well the moon is bright, the clouds flow, the sky is spread,
   the blue wind blows, and autumn is there.

Also a young man is in the well. Hating this man I turn away.
   But as I go on I come to pity him.

When I return and look into the well again, that young man is still
   there. I start to hate him again and turn away. But as I go
   on I come to long for him.

In the well the moon is bright, the clouds flow, the sky is spread,
   the blue wind blows, autumn reigns, and a young man stands
   there.

Cho Chi-hun

Born in 1920 in the South, he studied at Hyehwa College (now Tong-guk University) in Seoul and later taught at Koryŏ University. He was one of the "Southern Trio" who entered the literary world shortly before the end of the Second World War. Cho died in 1968. "The wooden fish" in the first poem is a round object used to keep time in chanting scriptures.

ANCIENT TEMPLE

Overcome by a stealthy slumber,
An altar boy

With the wooden fish in his hands,
Closes his eyes and nods.

While Amitābha and Bodhisattva
Smile, smile without words,

Along the western borders,
Under the blinding red sky,
Peonies fall, peonies fall.

MOUNTAIN HUT

By the closed brushwood door,
Petals tremble.

The hut, lapped by clouds,
Echoes the stream's limpid voice.

The orchid leaves shudder,
Wet by the sweet rain,

And the honey bees swing by
The sun-flared paper screen.

Stubborn rocks sit still,
Proud of their slick moss.

Amid a wind's faint ripples,
The ferns curl their tendrils.

Cho Pyŏng-hwa

Born in 1921, he taught mathematics in a high school before joining
the faculty of Kyŏnghŭi University.

ONE WINTER DAY

Between the boughs of a tall tree the sun rises like a persimmon
in the gray sky.

I will rise before sunrise and wait for the persimmon sun to climb
up the eastern sky below my window.

My room is perched up high like a magpie's nest.

Cold winds steal into my room, where I live through the chilly
winter.

The thermometer shows around 37 degrees.

I live on the warmth of the sun.

I look down on the rising sun from my bed perched like a mag-
pie's nest, wrapped in a soft quilt.

Like a crayon painting the beautiful persimmon sun mounts the
gray sky between the tall boughs, pouring its warmth on my
body.

THE TŎKSU PALACE

A butterfly reels away
from the trampled lawn by the lake.

A bronze seal spouts water from its mouth
in the garden of the marble building.

178

A tramp is taking a fitful nap
in the shadow of wistaria vines.

Wastepaper, cigarette butts, chewing gum
strewn on the ground by the Sunday crowd.

With dull movements
A weary old widow cleans up the mess.

Fading azaleas.
Disillusion.

A dreary feeling weighs upon
the peony garden in the Tŏksu Palace.

The trampled lawn by the lake—
little lances of gleaming light.

THE POND

Sultry summer days—

A pond forms in the field,
fish breed there under the willow.

Water plants in the cool shade of the tree;
fish swim leisurely below.

The smell of country wine from a village
by the pond where frogs croak.

Farmers of the village love this pond.

Silly water snakes also live there—
those cowardly creatures.

Flowers bloom, too,
on the clear water of the pond.

Page 33. 1) I have given reign dates for all rulers and, beginning with the Koryŏ period (918–1392), I have also given their birth–death dates.

Page 52. 1) Rahu is the god of solar eclipse. Ch'ŏyong was, for unknown reasons, considered a son of the god of solar eclipse.

Page 53. 2) The three calamities: of two kinds, major and minor. "The minor, appearing during a decadent world-period, are sword, pestilence, and famine; the major, for world destruction, are fire, water, and wind." Soothill and Hodous, A Dictionary of Chinese Buddhist Terms (SH: London, 1937), 69b.

3) The eight difficulties: the eight conditions in which it is difficult to see a Buddha or hear his law. SH, 41a.

4) The seven treasures: gold, silver, lapis lazuli, crystal, agate, rubies, and cornelian. SH, 11b-12a.

Page 54. 1) The Turks were supposed to have a little doll (puppet) on the shelves of their bakeries for decoration. During the thirteenth and fourteenth centuries, Korean kings married Mongol princesses, who brought to Korea thousands of court ladies, maids in waiting, and other servants. A certain number of Turks, who were Moslems, entered Korea at about the same time.

Page 56. 1) The fifteenth day of the seventh lunar month and the last day of the Lantern Festival. The festival is for the deliverance of hungry ghosts, often spoken of as the feast of all souls, from the Sanskrit, ullambana, "deliverance."

2) The fifteenth day of the eighth lunar month; according to the lunar calendar, it is the midautumn day.

Page 62. 1) According to the commentators, the word "duck" was used as a half-pejorative and half-coaxing epithet in the Koryŏ dynasty.

Page 72. 1) The brothers Po I and Shu Ch'i disapproved of the conquests by Chou of their overlord the Shang king. They retired to Shou-yang mountain, resolved "not to eat the corn of Chou," and died of starvation. Herbert

A. Giles, *Chinese Biographical Dictionary* (*BD*: Shanghai, 1898), 1657; *Shih chi* 61, 0179a-c (Chinese dynastic histories are quoted from the *Erh-shih-wu shih*, K'ai-ming edition, Shanghai, 1935).

Page 73. 1) Literally "red dust," but alludes to mundane life.

Page 74. 2) Alludes to the *Analects* XI, 25. While Tzu-lu, Jan Ch'iu, and Kung-hsi Hua desired power and politics, Tseng Hsi, in perhaps the most beautiful and at the same time most Taoistic passages in the *Analects*, expressed that what he desired was not a kingdom but a life in harmony with *li* ("rites"; "decorum"), with his fellow men, and with nature. "Tseng Hsi said, At the end of spring, when the making of the Spring Clothes has been completed, to go with five times six newly capped youths and six times seven uncapped boys, perform the lustration in the river I, take the air at the Rain Dance altars, and then go home singing." See Arthur Waley, *The Analects of Confucius* (London, 1949), p. 160.

3) Imaginary world created by T'ao Ch'ien (365–427), in his poem, entitled "Peach Blossom Fountain." See Herbert A. Giles, *Gems of Chinese Literature: Prose* (Shanghai, 1923), pp. 104-105.

4) *Analects* VI, 9; Waley, p. 117.

Page 85. 1) Mt. Wu-i is in Fukien and has thirty-six peaks.

2) Master Chu is Chu Hsi (1130–1200), who synthesized Sung Neo-Confucianism.

Page 88. 1) Sŏng Hon, 1535–1598.

2) Mr. Ko is Ko Kyŏng-myŏng (1533–1592).

Page 89. 3) The Office of Special Counselors, also called the Jade Hall, established in 1478.

Page 90. 4) A mountain range in Kweichou and Hunan.

Page 93. 1) Tally: token of delegated authority, made of jade, issued as credentials.

2) Upper tributary of the Han River.

3) Kung Ye (?–901–918) raised a rebellion against the Silla dynasty and named his state T'aebong. He occupied the area of modern Ch'ŏrwŏn.

4) Good administrator under the Emperor Wu (140–86 B.C.) of the Former Han dynasty. He died at about 108 B.C. He was governor of Huai-yang, the name of

which is identical with that of a town in Kangwŏn
Province in Korea. *BD*, 268; *Shih chi* 120, 0262c–
0263a; Burton Watson, tr., *Records of the Grand Historian of China*, II (New York, 1961), 343–352.

Page 94. 5) Lin Pu or Ho-ching (976–1028), a native of Ch'ien-t'ang in Chekiang, lived on a hill near the West Lake where he amused himself by growing plum trees and keeping cranes. *BD*, 1258; *Sung shih* 457, 5650a.

6) Famous mountain in Kiangsi. Su Shih and Li Po (701–762) sang of this mountain.

7) Both Mt. Tung and Mt. T'ai are in Shantung. Both were already mentioned in the *Book of Songs, Analects,* and *Mencius*. See *The Book of Songs* 300, 6; *Analects* III, 6; *Mencius* IIA, 2 and VIIA, 24.

8) Lu is the name of a state in which Confucius was born. This line is evidently didactic, implying that the teachings of Confucius are like an enormous mountain and that they are difficult to master.

Page 95. 9) An image of Maitreya Buddha carved on the cliff.

10) The Lu Cataract on Mt. Lu. Li Po wrote a poem, "Viewing the Cataract in the Lu Mountain." See Shigeyoshi Obata, "The Cataract of Luh (*sic*) Shan I and II," *The Works of Li Po* (New York, 1922), pp. 132–133.

11) Tradition has it that once upon a time four knights of Silla came here to admire the beauty of the Diamond Mountains and had not returned after three days, hence the name. There was a small peak to the south, on the top of which was a stone niche and on the north precipice of this peak were six Chinese characters in red ink which read: "We Are Going Toward the South."

Page 96. 12) Refers to a famous romance between Hongjang and the then Governor of Kangnŭng.

13) Two lines have been omitted at this point.

Page 97. 14) One of the Taoist classics. See *Chiu T'ang shu* 47, 3265b.

15) Compare the end of this poem with that of Su Shih's "The Red Cliff" (later *fu*): "And I dreamed that a Taoist priest, with feathery robe fluttering like an Immortal, passed by Lin Kao. Bowing low to me, he said, 'Has your visit to the Red Cliff been pleasant?' I asked

him his name but he lowered his head without replying. 'Alas!' I cried, 'Now I understand. Last night did you not fly over me and scream?' The Taoist priest glanced at me and smiled. Waking up in alarm, I opened the door and looked out. But I could see no one." See Cyril Drummond le Gros Clark, *The Prose-Poetry of Su Tung-P'o* (Shanghai, 1935), pp. 137–138.

Page 101. 1) The poem was written to praise the elegant life of Kim Sŏng-wŏn (1525–1598), which centered around the Sŏha Hall and Sigyŏng Arbor below Mount Star in South Chŏlla Province. Kim, together with his mother and wife, was killed by Japanese soldiers on a mountain behind the village of Tongbok. The villagers named the mountain Moho ("Guardian of the Mother").

Page 102. 2) The star Vega in the constellation of Lyra. These two lines allude to the beauty of the stream.

3) The Blue Gate is the southeast gate of Ch'ang-an ch'eng. In the time of Ch'in, Shao P'ing was enfeoffed as the Marquis of Tung-ling. But when the Han destroyed the Ch'in, he had to abandon his post and live by raising melons. The melons he raised were called either Tung-ling or Ch'ing-men melons.

Page 103. 4) Chou Tun-yi (1017–1073): one of the great Sung philosophers, author of the *Diagram of the Supreme Ultimate Explained*.

5) A fairy elucidated the Canon of Jade, supposed to be written by the legendary Yellow Emperor. *Wu-yüeh ch'un-ch'iu* (*Ssu-pu pei-yao* ed.) 6, 1b–2a.

6) Cannot locate this palace.

Page 104. 7) Su Shih (1036–1101) says in his preface to "The Red Cliff" that it was written in the seventh moon. See Le Gros Clark, *op. cit.*, p. 126: "In the autumn of the year Jen-hsü, when the seventh moon was on the wane, I, Su, was drifting with friends in a boat below the Red Cliff."

Page 105. 8) Hsü Yu was a princely man in the time of the legendary Emperor Yao. Knowing of his virtue and integrity, the Emperor suggested to him the possibility of leaving him the throne. Hsü Yu was too pure a man to listen to such an offer, and went to the river to cleanse his

183

ears. *BD*, 200; *Kao-shih chuan* (*Ssu-pu pei-yao* ed.) 1, 2b–3a.

Page 109. 1) Mt. Shang is in Shensi where "four gray-heads" retired from the world toward the close of the reign of the First Emperor of Ch'in, to emerge only upon the establishment of the Han dynasty. *BD*, 1881; *Shih chi* 55, 0172a; *Ch'ien Han shu* 40, 0459a–c.

2) Two lines have been omitted at this point.

Page 112. 1) He fought a sea battle against the invading Japanese Navy in 1592 in the Straits of Korea.

Page 113. 2) Refers to the poem No. 55 in the *Book of Songs* (Waley, p. 46): "Look at that little bay of the Ch'i,/ Its reeds so delicately waving./ Delicately fashioned is my Lord,/ As a thing cut, as a thing filed,/ As a thing chiseled, as a thing polished,/ Oh grace, oh elegance!"

Page 114. 3) *Analects XIV*, 11 (Waley, p. 182): "The Master said, To be poor and not resent it is far harder than to be rich, yet not presumptuous."

Page 114. 1) Who checked the march of the invading Japanese Army.

Page 115. 2) Two lines have been omitted at this point.

Page 116. 3) Two lines have been omitted at this point.

Page 117. 1) The three periods: past, present, and future in Buddhism.

Page 118. 2) The eight famous views of the Rivers Hsiao and Hsiang, two famous tributaries of the Yangtze.

3) Refers to the story of Ting Ling-wei (about second century), "a native of Liaotung, studied the black art on the Ling-hsü Mountain. At the expiration of a thousand years, he changed himself into a crane and flew home again and perched on the Hua-piao Gate, to find, as he mournfully expressed in verse: 'City and suburb as of old,/ But hearts that loved us long since cold.'" *BD*, 1938.

Page 120. 1) Cf. "The Return" of T'ao Ch'ien; Chang and Sinclair, *The Poems of T'ao Ch'ien* (Honolulu, 1953), p. 103: "When I see my doorway and house,/ I am happy, and I run./ The servants welcome me,/ And small children wait by the gate."

Page 129. 1) The office which helps the people in times of need, by

lending rice and cereals in the spring and letting the
people return them in the autumn.

2) Both are ancient Chinese sages who "neither abated
their high purpose nor abashed themselves," as Con-
fucius said of them. Cf. page 72, n. 1.

Page 135. 1) Here the poet is reminded of the poem, "The Fisher-
man," written about the middle of the third century
B.C. and traditionally attributed to Ch'ü Yüan. The
poem contains a famous admonition uttered by the
fisherman, who suggests that one should seek office in
good times and retire when the times are troubled.

Page 136. 2) The third and fourth lines refer to Wu Yüan, a native
of Ch'u. Denounced by his lord, Fu Ch'ai of the state
of Wu, he committed suicide. Fu was angry, caused his
body to be put into a leathern sack and thrown into
the Wu River, by the bank of which the people raised
a shrine to his memory. BD, 2358; Shih chi 66, 0183b–
0184b.

The fifth and sixth lines refer to Ch'ü Yüan (d. c. 288
B.C.), a minister in the state of Ch'u. He objected to
the use of force and was banished from the court. Dis-
tressed, he drowned himself in the Milo (or Ch'u)
River. BD, 503; Shih chi 84, 0209d–0210c; Burton
Watson, op. cit., I, 499–508.

Page 137. 3) Refers to a tradition that when the Emperor Shun
went to Mt. Li, he was given the field, and when he
went to Lei Stream, he was given a good place for fish-
ing. The lines therefore imply that one should lead an
old fisherman to an ideal place for fishing, following
the good example of the people in the time of Shun.
Shih chi 1, 0006a; Édouard Chavannes, Les Mémoires
Historiques de Se-ma Ts'ien, I (Paris, 1895), 72-74.

Page 139. 4) The Phoenix Pavilion is the royal palace.

5) Tradition says that the white hare pounds rice in the
moon.

6) Refers to the story told of the two legendary recluses,
Hsü Yu and Ch'ao-fu. When the Emperor Yao wished
to offer him the throne, Hsü Yu went to the river to
cleanse his ears because the Emperor told a pure man
such a story. When Ch'ao-fu saw Hsü Yu cleansing his
ears by the Ying River, he pulled his cow away from

the water, because he would not let his animal drink the water where Hsü Yu washed his ears. Cf. page 105, n. 8.

Page 140. 7) Tungt'ing Lake is in Hunan.

8) Refers to the tactics used by Li Su in a battle against Wu Yüan-chi (d. 817). Li captured the rebel's fortress by setting the geese and ducks free on a snowy night, thus camouflaging the marching of his troops. Here the poet reveals his hidden sorrow and asks himself when he will have a chance to avenge himself upon his political enemies. The reader should remember that the poet spent most of his life in exile due to party strife at court. See Chiu T'ang shu 133, 3441b–d; 145, 3470d–3471b; Hsin T'ang shu 154, 4011d–4012d; 214, 4127c–4128b. "The shame of soldier trees" refers to the following story. King of the Former Ch'in, Fu Chien (338–357–385), despite the stout opposition of his ministers, attacked Hsiao-wu ti (362–372–396) of the Eastern Chin and suffered a crushing defeat in 383. The retreating army feared ambush in every tree and tuft of grass and was scared by the sound of the wind and the whoop of the cranes. Indeed, the trees on Mt. Pa-kung looked like the Chin soldiers. See Chin shu 9, 1098a and 113, 1376c; Tzu-chih t'ung-chien (Peking, 1957) 104, 3301–3313 and 105, 3311–3312.

Page 141. 9) "Land of the fairies": in the original the place mentioned is the traditional Chinese elysium where only recluses and spirits reside.

10) The third and fourth lines refer to Yen Kuang, a contemporary of the Han Emperor Kuang-wu. He retired to Mt. Fu-ch'un and spent his life fishing. BD, 2468; Kao-shih chuan 3, 1a–2a; Hou Han shu 113, 0892c. The fifth and sixth lines refer to T'ai-kung (Lü Wang), who went into voluntary exile to escape the tyranny of the Shang king, Chou, and spent ten years fishing. King Wen found him upon the banks of Wei and carried him away to be his chief counselor. BD, 1862; Shih chi 32, 0123c–0124a; Chavannes, op. cit., IV (Paris, 1901), 34–40.

Page 142. 1) Five lakes and a smoky moon: an expression for "a carefree life amid Nature." Originally the Jade Emperor was the supreme deity of Taoism, but here it means the king.

2) The Palace of Twelve Pavilions: originally where the supreme deity of Taoism resides; but here it refers to the royal palace in Seoul.

Page 150. 1) Another version of this poem ends here.

2) I have chosen only a few lines from the remaining portion of the poem in a third version.

Page 151. 1) One line has been omitted at this point.

2) The allusion is to "Mr. Five Willows," a work of T'ao Ch'ien, in which T'ao created a type of a hermit scholar who scorns glory or profit and finds joy in elegant pleasures. Five willow trees are said to have surrounded his house, hence he is called "The Scholar of the Five Willows." See Chang and Sinclair, op. cit., p. 106.

3) Two lines have been omitted at this point.

4) The people in Seoul, having heard the evening bell in the Chongno Square on the fifteenth day of the first moon, would leave off whatever they were doing and go to the bridges in the capital and stamp on them. This was supposed to prevent a sickness of the feet.

Select Bibliography

An Ch'uk, *Kŭnjae chip* ("Collected Works of An Ch'uk"). Seoul, 1870.

Anonymous, *Haedong p'unga* ("Elegant Things of Korea"). Seoul, n.d.

Anonymous, *Kagok sŏn* ("Anthology of Korean Verse"). Seoul, 1913.

Anonymous, *Namhun t'aep'yŏng ka* ("Songs of Peace"). Seoul, c. 1801–1863.

Anonymous, *Siyong hyangak po* ("Music Book of Popular Songs": Tongbanghak yŏn'guso ed.). Seoul, 1954.

Chi Hŏn-yŏng, *Hyangga yŏyo sinsŏk* ("New Translations of Old and Middle Korean Poems"). Seoul, 1947.

Cho Yun-je, *Chosŏn siga sagang* ("History of Korean Poetry"). Seoul, 1937.

Cho Yun-je, *Hanguk siga ŭi yŏn'gu* ("Studies in Korean Poetry"). Seoul, 1948.

Ch'oe Nam-sŏn, *Sijo yuch'wi* ("Thematic Catalogue of Short Lyric Poems"). Seoul, 1928.

Chŏng Ch'ŏl, *Songgang kasa* ("Pine River Anthology"). Seoul, 1959.

Chŏng In-ji et al., *Koryŏ sa* ("History of the Koryŏ Dynasty": Tongbanghak yŏn'guso ed.). Seoul, 1955.

Chŏng Mong-ju, *Poŭn chip* ("Collected Work of Chŏng Mong-ju": Taedong munhwa yŏn'guwŏn ed.). Seoul, 1959.

Han Ch'i-yun, *Haedong yŏksa* ("History of Korea"). Seoul, 1911.

Hyŏngnyŏn Chŏng, *Kyunyŏ chŏn* ("Life of the Great Master Kyunyŏ": Ch'oe Nam-sŏn ed.). Seoul, 1954.

Iryŏn, *Samguk yusa* ("Remains of the Three Kingdoms": Ch'oe Nam-sŏn ed.). Seoul, 1954.

Kim Ch'ŏn-t'aek, *Ch'ŏnggu yŏngŏn* ("The Eternal Language of Green Hills"). Seoul, 1946.

Kim Pu-sik, *Samguk sagi* ("Historical Record of the Three Kingdoms": Chosŏn shigakkai ed.). Seoul, 1928.

Kim Sŏng-bae et al., *Chuhae kasa munhak chŏnjip* ("Annotated Anthology of Kasa Poems"). Seoul, 1961.

Kim Su-jang, *Haedong kayo* ("Songs of Korea"). Seoul, 1763.

Lee, Peter H., *Studies in the Saenaennorae: Old Korean Poetry*. Serie Orientale Roma XXII. Rome, 1959.

Lee, Peter H., *Kranich am Meer: koreanische Gedichte*. Munich, 1959.

Marcus, Richard, et al., *Korean Studies Guide*. Berkeley and Los Angeles, 1954.

No Sa-sin et al., *Sinjŭng Tongguk yŏji sŭngnam* ("Encyclopaedia of Korean Geography": Kojŏn kanhaeng hoe ed.). Seoul, 1958.

Pak Chun, *Akchang kasa* ("Words for Music"). Seoul, 1957.

Pak Hyo-gwan and An Min-yŏng, *Kagok wŏllyu* ("Source Book of Songs"). Seoul, 1876.

Pak In-no, *Nogye chip* ("Reedy Valley Anthology"). 1800, 1904.

Pak Yong-dae et al., *Chŭngbo munhŏn pigo* ("Korean Encyclopaedia": Kojŏn kanhaeng hoe ed.). Seoul, 1957.

Sim Kwang-se, *Haedong akpu* ("Words for the Bureau of Music"). Seoul, 1909.

Sŏng Hyŏn, *Akhak kwebŏm* ("Canon of Music"). Seoul, 1933.

Songgye yŏnwŏrong, *Kogŭm kagok* ("Ancient and Modern Songs"). 1776.

Yang Chu-dong, *Koga yŏn'gu* ("Studies in Old Korean Poetry"). Seoul, 1955.

Yang Chu-dong, *Yŏyo chŏnju* ("Studies in Middle Korean Poetry"). Seoul, 1954.

Yi Che-hyŏn, *Ikchae nan'go* ("Collected Works of Yi Che-hyŏn": Taedong munhwa yŏn'guwŏn ed.). Seoul, 1959.

Yun Sŏn-do, *Kosan yugo* ("Collected Works of Yun Sŏn-do"). 1796.

INDEX OF AUTHORS

191

INDEX OF FIRST LINES